ADIDAM

The True World-Religion
Given by
The Promised God-Man,
ADI DA SAMRAJ

The Ruchira Avatar,
Adi Da Samraj

ADIDAM

The True World-Religion
Given by
The Promised God-Man,

ADI DA SAMRAJ

Written and compiled under the direction of
THE RUCHIRA SANNYASIN ORDER OF ADIDAM RUCHIRADAM

THE DAWN HORSE PRESS
MIDDLETOWN, CALIFORNIA

NOTE TO THE READER

All who study the Way of Adidam or take up its practice should remember that they are responding to a Call to become responsible for themselves. They should understand that they, not Avatar Adi Da Samraj or others, are responsible for any decision they make or action they take in the course of their lives of study or practice.

The devotional, Spiritual, functional, practical, relational, cultural, and formal community practices and disciplines referred to in this book are appropriate and natural practices that are voluntarily and progressively adopted by members of the practicing congregations of Adidam (as appropriate to the personal circumstance of each individual). Although anyone may find these practices useful and beneficial, they are not presented as advice or recommendations to the general reader or to anyone who is not a member of one of the practicing congregations of Adidam. And nothing in this book is intended as a diagnosis, prescription, or recommended treatment or cure for any specific "problem", whether medical, emotional, psychological, social, or Spiritual. One should apply a particular program of treatment, prevention, cure, or general health only in consultation with a licensed physician or other qualified professional.

Adidam is formally authorized for publication by the Ruchira Sannyasin Order of Adidam Ruchiradam. (The Ruchira Sannyasin Order of Adidam Ruchiradam is the senior Spiritual and Cultural Authority within the formal gathering of formally acknowledged devotees of the Divine World-Teacher, Ruchira Avatar Adi Da Samraj.)

NOTE TO BIBLIOGRAPHERS: The correct form for citing Ruchira Avatar Adi Da Samraj's Name (in any form of alphabetized listing) is: Adi Da Samraj

Produced by the Avataric Pan-Communion of Adidam
in cooperation with the Dawn Horse Press

Printed in Canada

International Standard Book Number: 1-57097-160-9

Library of Congress Catalog Card Number: 2003111585

CONTENTS

Da
ADIDAM

INTRODUCTION

The Divine Intervention in Human Time

In the religious and Spiritual traditions of human history, a common theme of prophecy appears: When the world is in its darkest hour, when self-interest has become the governing principle of human life, when the connection to the Living Divine has seemed to disappear from human society, when the world itself is threatened by the always imminent possibility of global conflict and widespread natural disaster, there is to come a final and all-completing Revelation of the Divine in human form.

The religious and Spiritual traditions speak, each in their own language, of a Promised God-Man. These prophecies come out of the deep intuition, in every human heart, that there is something more than the temporary pleasures and inevitable sufferings of ordinary life. They come out of the longing for Divine Help, and the heart-certainty that such Divine Help will not be denied. It is in Love-response to this universal heart-longing and intuition that the Divine has Appeared in human form.

Avatar Adi Da's birth in Jamaica, New York, 1939, was the full and literal "Emergence" of the Divine in human time. For the first two years of life, association with a human body was no obstruction to His awareness of His Divine Condition. He has described in His Spiritual Autobiography, *The Knee Of Listening*, how, in His infancy, He existed in a Radiant State of Being full of profound Love-Bliss. As He first acquired language, Avatar Adi Da described this Reality as the "Bright".

Later in Avatar Adi Da's childhood, there was also a forceful process of overwhelming Energy, pressing down into His head and throat—a process He described as the "Thumbs". His human body-mind was going through the process of combining at the cellular level with the Love-Blissful "Bright" Force in Which He had existed freely as an infant. All of this was necessary for Him to be equipped for His later Spiritual Work.

Through the human Birth of Avatar Adi Da, the "Bright" Divine Reality and Condition has been tangibly drawn down into this humble realm, for the Spiritual Blessing and Divine Awakening of human beings. This is the nature of the "Avatar"—the Divine One Who has "crossed down" from the Unmanifest into the manifest condition for the sake of liberating beings. The Appearance of Avatar Adi Da Samraj in this world is the fulfillment of the universal prophecy of the Promised God-Man. He has come to found a new tradition which He Offers to all—a religion based on the direct and present relationship to the Divine Incarnate—the true world-religion of Adidam.

The Eternal Relationship

In its essence, Adidam, the Way of life Given by Avatar Adi Da, is the devotional and (in due course) Spiritual *relationship* with Avatar Adi Da.

In any ordinary relationship, each of us tends to presume a "me" and a "someone else"—two separate entities interacting with one another. The relationship with Adi Da Samraj is of a different kind. He is the Divine Avatar and He is, therefore, not an "other". He is, in fact, our true Nature—the true Nature of every thing and every one, miraculously appearing via a particular human form.

Avatar Adi Da points out that each of us is *actively presuming* separation. And it is precisely this *presumption* of existing as a separate being that makes the apparent "difference" between each individual being and everyone and everything else. This presumption is the essence of suffering—leaving no recourse in the face of mortality and all the heart-breaking possibilities of separate existence. Avatar Adi Da is Revealing the way beyond the false presumption of separateness. He is here to awaken all human beings to What is inherently Non-Separate—to the Divine Condition, the "Bright" Spiritual Reality that is Incarnate in and as His human Form.

This profound recognition of His Divine Person and Function initiates the devotional relationship to Him that is the foundation of Adidam.

Avatar Adi Da writes, in His principal Scriptural Text, *The Dawn Horse Testament Of The Ruchira Avatar*:*

I Am The "Bright"—Itself.

This "Brightness" Speaks.

The "Bright" Is Born As This, My Avataric Body-Mind.

My Divine Spiritual Descent Upon the body-mind Of My Devotee—As The "Thumbs"—Is My Avataric Divine Means.

All This Was Given From The Avataric Birth Of This, My Bodily (Human) Divine Form.

Indeed, These Words—The "Bright" and The "Thumbs"—Were Generated By Me As An Infant.

I Am Uttering To You The Revelation That Was Present At My Birth and In My Infancy—and Nothing Whatsoever Has Been Added To It or Taken Away From It.

Nothing In The Human Experience Of This, My Avataric Body-Mind, Has Modified My Revelation or limited It In The Slightest.

My Avatarically-Given Revelation Is A Divine Spiritual Revelation For The Sake Of all beings.

Therefore, Heart-Recognize Me, and Heart-Respond To Me.

Turn To Me. Receive Me. Constantly Know Me.

If You Do This, You Will Be Certain Of The Truth I Am Telling You.

*In *The Dawn Horse Testament*, Avatar Adi Da employs a unique scriptural convention of capitalization, in which the overwhelming majority of words are capitalized, and only those words that indicate the egoic (or dualistic) point of view are left lower-cased. This capitalization convention is in itself a Teaching device, intended to communicate His fundamental Revelation that "There Is Only Real God", and that only the ego (or the dualistic or separative point of view) prevents us from living and Realizing that Truth.

The Three Great Principles Of All Truth

In this brief Essay, written in July 2003, Avatar Adi Da elucidates the perfect Truth of Non-Separateness that He has Realized and Revealed. Together, these three Principles Reveal a world-view of utter Unity: first, the Indivisible Unity of Reality (the Divine Self-Condition of all beings and things), second, the Unity of the world, or the cosmos (and the world's Non-"difference", in its True Self-Condition, from the Divine Reality), and, third, the Unity of each individual psycho-physical entity with the world, and its Non-separation from the Divine Reality. He describes this Truth as the "Reality-based" foundation of His Offering of the true world-religion of Adidam.

I. The Divine Principle of Indivisibility: Reality (Itself) is Inherently Indivisible (One and Divine and Un-conditional and Absolute)

II. The Universal (or Cosmic) Principle of Unity and Non-"Difference": The world (or the conditionally manifested cosmos) is Inherently a Unity (Which, in and As its True Self-Condition, is Inherently Non-"different" from the One and Indivisible and Absolute and Un-conditional Divine Reality)

III. The psycho-physical Principle of Non-Separateness: The individual psycho-physical entity is Inherently Non-separate from the world-Unity (or the Inherently Unified cosmic Totality, Which is Whole and Universal) and, also, Inherently Non-separate from the Inherently Indivisible Divine Reality (or the One and Conscious Light That Is the One and Only Self-Condition of all-and-All)

These Three Principles, Proposed by Me, are (Effectively) an Integrated Whole and Single Proposition. They (Together) Comprise the philosophical (and Reality-Based, and Reality-Realization-Based) Foundation for the Only-by-Me Revealed and Given Way of Adidam (Which is the One and Only by-Me-Revealed and by-Me-Given Way of the Heart). And They are, also, the Right and True Basis (and the Right and True Measure) for the Correct (and, inevitably, intellectually Liberating) Evaluation of any and all possible propositions of philosophical import made (now, or in the future, or in any time and place at all) by any one (or any school or tradition) at all.

Revealing the True World-Religion of Adidam

Throughout His Life-Revelation, Adi Da Samraj has undergone transformational Events in His human body, each of which magnified His Power to Manifest the "Bright" in this world. The first was His Submission to embrace the ordinary human life and allow His awareness of the "Bright" to fade, in order to learn and transcend the human situation. He made this Submission at the age of two, in a spontaneous Gesture of Love toward those around Him. Thus began a nearly thirty-year Ordeal of learning, and going beyond, all levels of human experience (both ordinary and "Spiritual"), until, in 1970, He Re-Awakened most perfectly to His native "Bright" Condition.

Beginning in 1972, Avatar Adi Da spent many years Teaching devotees and Addressing their doubts, questions, and sufferings. Even in the midst of their genuine efforts to practice the Spiritual Way He was Offering, they tended to fall back on habits that turned them away from Communion with Him. He engaged every kind of "Skillful Means" to help His devotees feel and understand the force of their commitment to the separate self, and to draw them into moment to moment Communion with Him.

In 1986, after 14 years of this intensive Teaching-Submission, Avatar Adi Da suffered a death-like Swoon, in which His Teaching Function was spontaneously relinquished, and a new phase of His Divine Work began. This Great Yogic Event was the beginning of Avatar Adi Da's full Avataric Divine Self-"Emergence" into the world.

Now Avatar Adi Da's body-mind was utterly Submitted to His own "Bright" Condition, and He began to "shed" His Submission to the necessities of dealing with devotees' egoic limitations and resistance. He Stood Firm in the "Bright", requiring all who approached Him to do so on the basis of right recognition of Him and right conformity to His Instruction.

Avatar Adi Da's Divine Blessing-Work now began in full. The "Bright" had acquired His body-mind down "to the toes", Transforming His human Vehicle such that it Communicated His Spiritual Transmission even more potently. His devotees could now feel clearly that Avatar Adi Da's Work was a Blessing of all beings. He was not just Working with a limited number of people for the sake of establishing His Teaching in the world. He was bringing His Divine Spiritual Transmission into the entire realm of physical appearances, Working to awaken all to the Divine Reality, and to bring the most benign changes and forces possible into human history.

On April 12, 2000, at Lopez Island (in the Northwest of the United States), Avatar Adi Da underwent another extraordinary Yogic death, in which He suddenly and spontaneously Ascended to His Pure "Bright" State infinitely Above the conditional worlds. Arising from that profoundly Ascended Swoon, He re-associated with His body-mind only down to "the brows", the Yogic place of contact just sufficient to maintain His connection to active bodily life.

Since the Lopez Island Event, I have never Re-Integrated with the physical to the extent that was previously the case (before that Event). Such Re-Integration simply did not occur.

Lopez Island, 2000

I Stand Where I Am.
I am not fixed here.
I have a "View" here, but I am not "of" the physical domain.
I Am here, it seems, for now. . . .
I Am the "Bright".
I Am the Means.
I Am the Realization.

—Avatar Adi Da Samraj
The Knee Of Listening

Avatar Adi Da is no longer Submitted to the world of ordinary egos in order to create Instruction in the Way of Adidam. That immense Labor of three decades has been recorded for all time in His twenty-three "Source-Texts", the Divine Scripture of Adidam. Now, Avatar Adi Da lives simply to Grant His silent Blessing-Regard to the entire world and to receive those who have formally prepared themselves to approach Him directly for the sake of His Spiritual Blessing.

Beyond the Cultic Tendency

Avatar Adi Da has always been extremely critical of what He calls "the cultic tendency" in human beings, or the hyped enthusiasm that groups of individuals generate around an object of their fascination. This cultic tendency, He points out, has nothing to do with the true process of Guru-devotion, and nothing to do with the Way of Adidam. In a key writing which He calls His "First Word", He describes how the real practice of the relationship to Him requires profound heart-recognition of Him as the Divine Person, Revealed in human Form. This recognition is a Gift. It has nothing to do with mere belief, or the kind of cultic enthusiasm that tries to make others believe what you believe.

The heart-recognition of Avatar Adi Da Samraj, awakened at the root of the being, engenders deep devotion, love, and gratitude to Him—and a natural tolerance for all others. This inherently ecstatic heart-recognition of Avatar Adi Da Samraj is the single authentic foundation for the practice of Adidam. As Avatar Adi Da describes here, such recognition moves one out from the cultic tendency to try to "encircle", or hold Him to oneself, or to presume that His Spiritual Gifts are a "commodity" that could be acquired. True devotional recognition of Him has the opposite effect. It is ego-transcending, a process that moves you to Him beyond your own separative ego, or self-"center". As Avatar Adi Da firmly states here, He is not interested in being the "man in the middle" of a group of cultic worshippers. He looks for the signs of real integrity in His devotees, the signs that they are practicing "Satsang", the devotional turning to Him that is genuinely transforming, rather than merely making gestures in His direction.

The true devotional and Spiritual relationship to Me is not separative (or merely "inward"-directed), nor is it a matter of attachment to Me as a mere (and, necessarily, limited) human being (or a "man in the middle")—for, if My devotee indulges in ego-bound (or self-referring and self-serving) attachment to Me as a mere human "other", My Divine Nature (and, therefore, the Divine Nature of Reality Itself) is not (as the very Basis for religious and Spiritual practice in My Company) truly devotionally recognized and rightly devotionally acknowledged. And, if such non-recognition of Me is the case, there is no truly ego-transcending devotional response to My Avatarically-Born and Avatarically Self-Revealed (and Self-Evidently Divine) Presence and Person—and, thus, such presumed-to-be "devotion" to Me is not devotional heart-Communion with Me, and such presumed-to-be "devotion" to Me is not Divinely Liberating. Therefore, because the true devotional (and, thus, truly devotionally Me-recognizing and, on that basis, truly devotionally to-Me-responding) relationship to Me is entirely a counter-egoic (and truly and only Divine) discipline, it does not (if rightly and truly practiced) become a "cult" (nor does it support the "cultic" tendency of Man).

The true devotional practice of Satsang with Me is (inherently) expansive—or anti-contractional, or anti-constrictive, or decompressive, or pro-relational. Thus, the self-contracting (or separate and separative) self-"center" is neither the motive nor the source of Satsang with Me. In true Satsang with Me, the egoic "center" is always already undermined as a "center" (or a presumed separate, and actively separative, entity). The Principle of true Satsang with Me is Me—Beyond (and not "within"—or, otherwise, supporting) the self-referring ego-"I". . . .

The Great Secret of My Avatarically-Born bodily (human) Divine Form and Person, and of My Avatarically Self-Transmitted Divine Spiritual Blessing-Work (now, and forever hereafter)—and, therefore, the Great Secret of the only-by-Me Revealed and Given Way of Adidam—Is that I am not the "man in the middle", but I Am Reality Itself, I Am the Only One Who Is, I Am That Which Is Always Already The Case, I Am the Non-Separate (Avatarically Self-Revealed, and Self-Evidently Divine) Person (or One and Very Divine Self, or One and True Divine Self-Condition) of all-and-All (Beyond the ego-"I" of every one, and of all, and of All). . . .

I Am That One and Only and Non-Separate One. And—As That One, and Only As That One—I Call all human beings to heart-recognize Me, and (on that basis) to heart-respond to Me with right, true, and full devotion (demonstrated by Means of formal practice of the only-by-Me Revealed and Given Way of Adidam—Which Is the One and Only by-Me-Revealed and by-Me-Given Way of the Heart).

—Avatar Adi Da Samraj
"First Word"

The Promised God-Man Is Here

The surpassing Gift of the Ruchira Avatar, Adi Da, to all human beings is His Incarnate human Form, through which He has Tested and Proven every detail of the Way He has Given. In His Submission to "Learn" and to "Teach" humankind, Avatar Adi Da Samraj has Descended into the depths of the mortal life and struggle. At the same time, His Purity has been absolute. He has never been other than He Is—the "Bright" Divine Being, Incarnate here.

The human Form of Avatar Adi Da is perfectly continuous with His Infinite Divine Form. Real God is here in the bodily manifested Form of Adi Da Samraj, here to be recognized and worshipped in His Purity, His Freedom, His "Bright" Spirit-Force of Divine Love-Bliss. He is Shining Down from Above and Beyond, at the core of the manifest worlds. The Power of His Avataric Form to Transform and Purify the body-mind of His devotee whose entire being is turned to Him cannot be measured. Even the smallest gesture of real heart-turning has profound effects, because every act of such turning loosens the grip of ego, the act of presuming separation. Without that turning, the presumption of separateness is constantly active at every level of the being. It is the Divine Blessing, the Transmission of the "Bright"—Granted by the Ruchira Avatar, Adi Da Samraj—that releases the knot at the heart and Illumines the being.

Speaking to His devotees in *The Knee Of Listening*, Avatar Adi Da has written, "The Worship Of The 'Bright' Must Be Established In This conditional Realm." Such is the Way of Adidam—the Worship of the "Bright" Divine Reality forever—Revealed in Person, through the human Form of the Ruchira Avatar, Adi Da Samraj.

To practice Adidam is not a merely personal matter. Adidam is the infinitely great Process of participation in the Avataric Work of the Divine Master, Adi Da Samraj. This is right worship of Him—to provide for His Blessing of beings, to devote all one's actions to service of His Blessing-Intention, and thus to allow Him to

fulfill the Purpose of His Avataric Birth. Avatar Adi Da Samraj is here for everyone, without exception. He is Responding, as He says, to the yearning of the very molecules of existence. His Divine Presence is Pressing Down into the heart of the world. People everywhere are feeling Him profoundly, long before they know His Name.

Having truly found Him, one cannot keep silent, but only respond to His Calling:

Tell every one That I Am here!—As It Was (By Ancients) Always Promised I Would Be!

Now (and Forever Hereafter), My Every Devotee Is The God That I Am here To Find.

Now (and Forever Hereafter), I Am The God My Every Devotee Is here To Realize.

—Avatar Adi Da Samraj
Aham Da Asmi

The Ruchira Sannyasin Order of Adidam Ruchiradam

The Ruchira Sannyasin Order is the body of Avatar Adi Da's most advanced devotees who have chosen to consecrate their lives utterly to Him and His Way—by embracing the life of formal renunciation, in the circumstance of perpetual retreat. Avatar Adi Da has designated the Ruchira Sannyasin Order as the senior cultural authority within the gathering of His devotees—both during and after His physical Lifetime. Thus, it is the unique responsibility of the Ruchira Sannyasin Order to function both as the extension of His Sacred Authority and as His Instrumentality (or the collective human "conduit" for His Spiritual Blessing).

The Ruchira Sannyasin Order of Adidam Ruchiradam is (and must always be) the most senior gathering of (necessarily, formal) practitioners of the Way of Adidam—and the hierarchically central, and most senior (but entirely renunciate, and non-managerial), functioning cultural authority among, and in relation to, all the (necessarily, formal) practitioners of the Way of Adidam. . . .

All the present members and all the future members of the Ruchira Sannyasin Order of Adidam Ruchiradam are Called and Empowered (by Me) to Function (collectively) as the principal and most senior (physically living, human) Instruments of My forever Blessing Work, and, by their unique (and uniquely authoritative) cultural service (simply by Wisdom-word and practicing example), to provide all other practitioners of the Way of Adidam with the principal Good Company (of fellow devotees) that is necessary for the inspiration and guidance of their practice of the Way of Adidam.

—Avatar Adi Da Samraj
"The Orders of My True and Free Renunciate Devotees"

Right Human Life Must Transcend the Materialist "Culture" of Death*

An Essay by Avatar Adi Da Samraj

In this Essay, Avatar Adi Da addresses the culture of materialistic thought in its root-presumption. First, He describes the fundamental situation of one who is identified with the gross (physical) body—the inevitability of death. Then, He describes how the effort to gain mere "knowledge" completely misses the point of the bondage that materialism itself imposes. The opposites of "problem" and "solution" perpetuate bondage. Only the Revelation of Truth—the response to Indivisible Reality—can free human beings from their mortal philosophy. This is the foundation understanding of Adidam—the Way of heart-recognition and heart-response to Avatar Adi Da Samraj.

"Consider" This.

The gross (physical) human body is, literally, a death machine. It is not merely, in fact (or as a result of some future conditions), going to die—it is (now, and from its beginnings) patterned to die. Indeed, it intends to die, and even makes itself die. It progressively brings itself to death.

Thus, from the moment of its birth (and even from its conception), the gross (physical) human body—in and of itself—is not about life, but about death. Therefore, to truly be about life requires a unique and profound disposition.

*This Essay is included in *Real God Is The Indivisible Oneness Of Unbroken Light* and *The Basket Of Tolerance*.

Having been born in gross (physical) bodily form, you (in reaction to the perceived and conceived imposition of limited and threatening conditions) become bound to the gross point of view of identification with the physical body in and of itself, as a separate entity. As a result of that reactive (or self-contracting) gesture of identification, you are (thereby) bound to the natural program of the physical body, which is death itself. Consequently, you are reactively enacting a separate and separative life that is entirely about the disposition of death and the self-reinforcing reaction to the natural inevitability of death.

In this "late-time" (or "dark" epoch), the common human world is characteristically (and altogether) invested in this gross disposition of identification with the seemingly separate gross (physical) body—and, therefore, the common human world is becoming overwhelmed with the "culture" of death.

This "culture" of death (which is, in actuality, an anti-culture) is not merely the result of some kind of philosophical "taste" for the idea of death. Most fundamentally, the "culture" of death arises from the universal ego-act of identification with apparently separate existence and (in particular) with gross (physical) existence as the separate physical (human) body. The inevitable result of this ego-act is that consciousness becomes identified with the patterned "program" of death and fails to generate (or even allow for the possibility of) any greater philosophy.

All of this is not to say that human beings should adopt the disposition of wanting to somehow separate (or dissociate) from the gross (physical) body. The necessary transformation in individual and collective human culture will come about only through the Divine-Grace-Given Awakening to the responsive (and counter-egoic, or non-contractive—rather than reactive and self-contracting) disposition. The responsive (and participatory, and ego-surrendering) disposition inherently transcends the body, and (thereby) inherently transcends death. In that case, a different kind of individual and collective human culture is made possible. That culture is the death-transcending culture of life itself—which is (necessarily) a culture of Spiritual practice, and (ultimately) the culture of Divine life. Unfortunately for all, it is that very culture of human, Spiritual, and Divine life which has now been propagandized out of the realm of possibility by the dogma (or thoroughly reductionist point of view) of scientific materialism (and everything that flows from that benighted point of view).

The dogma of scientific materialism cannot be effectively countered by conventional (or merely exoteric) religion—because conventional (or merely exoteric) religion is based on a calling to embrace a culture of beliefs that (whether or not the beliefs themselves are truly valid) cannot really be upheld (or supported) by the presumed-to-be-separate body (or egoic body-mind) that would want to believe in it. The naive (and even utopian and ego-immortalizing) tenets of conventional (or merely exoteric) religion cannot be really and thoroughly believed by the ego (or the separate and separative body-mind), because the ego (which is inherently reactive and self-contracting) is grossly and materialistically body-bound (and the gross physical body itself is naturally programmed to produce death).

Thus, falsely upheld (or ego-bound) religion is (like scientific materialist philosophy) a symptomatic characteristic of gross ego-"culture". Indeed, it is, principally, the combination of grossly bound (scientific materialist) anti-culture with widespread exoteric religious fanaticism that has produced the "dark" realities of this "late-time".

There is no objection to be made to science itself, simply as a mode of enquiry. Science itself can, of course, be a very useful and beneficial human enterprise. The fault arises when the enterprise of scientific enquiry becomes associated with a "culture" of false presumptions—in particular, a philosophical tradition of materialism (which aggressively insists that gross physical "matter" is the "only" reality). The (necessarily, reactive) philosophy of materialism is the same phenomenon (on the collective scale) as the reactive self-identification with the apparently separate gross (physical) body (on the individual scale). The presumption of "matter-only"—or the subjective identification with the material body—is (inherently) a dying thing, a philosophy of the dead.

The philosophical proclamation of materialism inherently implies everything "dark"—death as the meaningless ending to temporary life, the meaningless "creativity" of an "accidental" universe, the ultimate futility of all human effort and purpose, and so on. In the common social sphere, much propaganda (based on inherited exoteric religious doctrine) is communicated to the generality of humankind, with the intention of aligning the collective to the conventional purposes of social morality—but the exoteric religious doctrines used to justify conventional social morality (or even truly human integrity) are not at all upheld by the "culture" of scientific materialism. In fact, exactly the opposite is the case.

Whenever phenomena of an extraordinary (and, especially, Spiritual or Divine) kind (relating to human experience) are discussed or referred to, the "culture" of scientific materialism insists on explaining these phenomena in terms of a gross psycho-physical description of the human entity. That reductionist disposition simply does not (and cannot fully) understand reality. That reductionist disposition is burdened with its own self-adopted prejudices about reality—the prejudices of materiality-only, self-identification with the gross (physical) body, and so on. Any disposition that identifies with separate existence as a gross (physical) entity is (inherently) associated with a "culture" of death, a "culture" of bondage—an unillumined "culture" that fails to understand reality rightly, precisely because of its prejudiced point of view relative to reality itself.

Thus, the "culture" of scientific materialism is identified with a fundamental (and, in its implications, disastrous) misunderstanding of the nature of reality.

The right understanding of the nature of reality (or of Reality Itself—Which Is One, and Only, and Inherently Indivisible) has been Communicated by Me in many forms—as epitomized by My Essay "The Three Great Principles Of All Truth" [see pp. 12-13]. I have Given that Essay (and all My related Communications) to humankind as a Gift of necessary education, for the Sake of the "Brightening" of the entire human world.

It must come to be recognized that the underlying "faith" (common in this "late-time") that "It is the word of science—and, therefore, it is true" is exactly equivalent to the medieval "faith" that "It is the word of the church—and, therefore, it is true." In both cases, what is (or was) being promulgated is doctrine—not Truth. And, whatever the prevailing doctrine may be, it is always kept in place by institutionalized means, to be reinforced (by propagandistic authoritarian efforts) over and over again. In this "late-time" (or "dark" epoch), the language of science is commonly associated with the idea of authority—but no form of institutionalized conventional knowledge is (or can be) true authority. Only Truth (Itself)—Which Is Reality Itself—Is true authority.

If Reality Itself is not rightly understood (in other words, if you do not have right philosophy as the basis for knowledge), then knowledge becomes ignorance—a source of bondage, of self-deluded life, and of suffering.

Therefore, the false philosophy of scientific materialism must be transcended. Only the transcending of false (or ego-based) philosophy allows for the possibility of right life—which is, ultimately, the true (or esoteric, rather than the conventional, or merely exoteric) religious (or Spiritual and Divine) life.

The prevailing approach to the investigation of "reality" was succinctly expressed in a speech given by Grayson Kirk, the president of Columbia College when I began My studies there (in 1957). In that speech, Grayson Kirk said, "At Columbia, we won't teach you how to be happy, but we will teach you how to think." Ultimately, that statement indicates that, from his (or the conventional academician's) point of view, the educational process is not purposed to discover the Truth, but (instead) it is purposed to develop the conceptual mechanism for relating (or reacting) to the drama of the perceived and conceived natural world of contradictions.

The mind is a beginningless and endless program of opposites. Therefore, the use of the mind—no matter how finely honed—never, in and of itself, results in Happiness. And, concomitantly, the use of the mind never, in and of itself, results in Truth.

Happiness, or Truth, or Reality Itself, is not the "point" of "point of view".

The pattern of opposites (or contractions) is simply a play upon "point of view". Therefore, no Truth—and, also, no Happiness—

ever comes as a result of any engagement in (or any study, quantification, or analysis of) that pattern. To involve yourself in the pattern of opposites is to commit yourself to endless struggle and purposeless drama.

In the common ego-world, conflict (or the confrontation of opposites) is enshrined as a "value"—or, indeed, as the chief means of stimulating oneself to remain "interested" in life. Indeed, conflict itself is made to seem irreducible, or a quality of life that is inherently the case—with the devastating (though almost entirely unrecognized) consequence that Truth (or the right, true, and final resolution of any and all conflict) is, in effect, held to be impossible to find. This is so because "point of view" is held to be the ultimate "value"—and points of view are always (and perpetually) in opposition to each other.

The ego-"culture" of this "late-time" (or "dark" epoch) is all a play upon the most limited possible point of view: identification with the gross (physical) body—and, therefore, identification with a natural (or, otherwise, presumed) process that inevitably leads to death. The entire world of the "late-time" is bound to this philosophy of utter "darkness".

Right human life is not a matter of any kind of "dialogue" (or, really, competition) between different points of view. Right human life is a matter of Truth. And, therefore, right human life is a matter of transcending "point of view", contradiction, and conflict.

Right human life must be based on Truth—and, therefore, on rightly understanding Reality Itself. Without such right understanding, humankind is merely participating in a tragic error—an error that results in perpetual conflict and death.

For the Sake of right understanding (and Divine Self-Realization) of Reality Itself, Truth Itself, and Happiness Itself, I have Given My Avataric Divine Wisdom-Revelation to the entire world. By Means of My Avataric Divine Wisdom-Revelation (and My Avataric Divine Self-Revelation, and My Avataric Divine Spiritual Self-Transmission), humankind (now, and forever hereafter) has the possibility of understanding and transcending the terrible tendencies of this "dark" time and all future time.

Therefore—for the Sake of all and All—"Consider" This.

Five Fundamentals of the True World-Religion of Adidam

The Five Fundamentals of Adidam described in this book are a means to comprehend the elements of the Way that Avatar Adi Da Samraj has Given.

The first fundamental is the essential practice of Ruchira Avatara Bhakti Yoga—the practice of devotion to Avatar Adi Da Samraj that is the foundation of the entire process of Adidam.

The second fundamental is the re-patterning of one's life through form and discipline, which provides the stable foundation for that devotion to deepen.

The third fundamental deals with the technical practices related to attention and energy which support the fundamental practice of devotion to Avatar Adi Da.

The fourth fundamental is the great process of receiving Avatar Adi Da's Spiritual Transmission. This is the Gift of Avatar Adi Da's Ruchira Shaktipat—or His Spiritual Transmission ("Shaktipat") of His own Divine Spiritual "Brightness" ("Ruchira").

The fifth (and final) fundamental of Adidam is Ruchira Shaktipat Yoga, the Spiritually Awakened practice of devotion to Avatar Adi Da. By means of His Divine Grace, this eventually becomes the "Perfect Practice" of devotion to Him, and (ultimately) Divine Enlightenment.

In this "late-time" (or "dark" epoch), human beings are becoming more and more deeply disenchanted with conventional religion and conventional "answers". . . .

Adidam is not a conventional religion.
Adidam is not a conventional way of life.
Adidam is about the transcending of the ego-"I".
Adidam is about the Freedom of Divine Self-Realization.

Adidam is not based on mythology or belief.
Adidam is a "reality" practice.
Adidam is a "reality consideration", in which the various modes of egoity are progressively transcended.

Adidam is a universally applicable Way of life.
Adidam is for those who will choose it, and whose hearts and intelligence fully respond to Me and My Offering.
Adidam is a Great Revelation, and It is to be freely and openly communicated to all.

—Avatar Adi Da Samraj
Ruchira Tantra Yoga

FIRST FUNDAMENTAL

Ruchira Avatara Bhakti Yoga

The Practice of Devotion to the Ruchira Avatar, Adi Da Samraj

The entire life of My devotee must be Ruchira Avatara Bhakti Yoga, or the always present-time devotional Yoga of direct (and directly and immediately ego-transcending) relationship to Me.

—Avatar Adi Da Samraj
Da Love-Ananda Gita

Devotion is heart-surrender (or response) to That Which is recognized to be great, profound, and Divine. This is so for an individual in any religious tradition. The supreme form of devotion, confessed in the esoteric Spiritual traditions, is devotion to a Master, or Guru—a Spiritually-Awakened being who is qualified to awaken his or her own Spiritual Realization in others. Since ancient times, it has been recognized by esoteric Spiritual practitioners that it is the Master's Spiritual Transmission that awakens the devotee.

Although it is continuous with this esoteric essence of the entire Great Tradition of religious and Spiritual endeavor, the practice of Guru-devotion in Adidam is unique. Devotion to Avatar Adi Da is based on recognizing and responding to Him as the Revealed Divine Person—Real God before your eyes. To recognize Him as the Divine Intervention in human time is the most ecstatic, life-transforming discovery. It is a Gift, not an effort. In that recognition, the being is moved to Him in a single, spontaneous, self-forgetting gesture.

When I am heart-recognized, then there is no longer any mental effort to grasp (or comprehend, or understand) either the conditional reality or the Unconditional Reality.

When I am heart-recognized (and the ego-self of body-mind is, thereby, forgotten in Me), then Only I Am Standing There—Unmediated, in-Filling body-mind from head to toe (from Infinitely Above to Deep Below). . . .

When My devotee practices the Way of Adidam on the basis of heart-recognition of Me, he or she is inherently in heart-Communion with Me. . . .

In that State of Ecstatic Inclusiveness with Me, the whole body-mind follows the heart, in devotional (ego-surrendering, ego-forgetting, and, always more and more, ego-transcending) response to Me (in and As My Avatarically-Born bodily human Divine Form and Person).

—Avatar Adi Da Samraj
Hridaya Rosary

Two Esoteric Laws

The practice of devotion to Avatar Adi Da is based on two esoteric laws:

1. You become what you meditate on.

Putting your attention on something is a very powerful act. When you fix your attention on something over time, it influences you profoundly, and you create a habit-pattern. This principle works to your advantage in the practice of devotion to Avatar Adi Da. Because the "Bright" is Shining in (and as) Avatar Adi Da's human body, turning attention and energy to Him awakens direct Communion with His "Bright" Divine Condition Itself.

2. Whatever is not used becomes obsolete.

The other side of the first esoteric law is that whatever you do not put your attention on tends to fall away. By doing this practice of turning to Avatar Adi Da, you relinquish self-oriented and loveless habit-patterns of thought, feeling, and action. Thus, these ego-patterns gradually become obsolete, and you are more and more awakened to the constant process of heart-Communion with Him.

The "programs" of egoic habit do not persist unless you give them your life-energy and attention. If you give your life-energy and attention to Me (instead), then all your egoic "programs" will, Ultimately, become obsolete and (literally) vanish. That Is the Divine Truth and the Divine Law.

You reinforce (or become) whatever you put your attention on (or to). Therefore, if you make Me the Object of your attention, all the other "things" of attention (which have no permanence) will dissolve.

If you (merely, or inherently searchlessly) turn to Me, the Virtue That I Am will Prove Itself. Therefore, I will Prove Myself to you, without your egoic effort, if you will do this simple (devotionally, and inherently, counter-egoic) turning to Me.

—Avatar Adi Da Samraj
Da Love-Ananda Gita

"Ego-Transcending" Devotion

The practice of devotion to Avatar Adi Da is an "ego-transcending" process—a process of going beyond the ego. In Avatar Adi Da's Teaching, the term "ego" means something very specific. It means the sense of being a separate self, an "I" over against others.

How does this sense of separation, of separate identity, arise? Avatar Adi Da Teaches that it arises through our own activity—an activity that He calls "self-contraction".

The True Nature (or Self-Condition) of everyone and everything is the "Bright". But through our own act of self-contraction (which is habitual and largely unconscious), we create the sense of a separate, limited, mortal self (or ego). We identify with a human body-mind. And in so doing, we cut ourselves off from awareness of the Free and unlimited Condition of Love-Bliss-Light—the "Bright". The ego (the conditional self) is not an entity, a mere "fact" of existence. The ego is an activity—something that each of us is doing. Avatar Adi Da has often illustrated the nature of this self-contracting activity by holding up an open hand, which is freely and directly related to the world, and then contrasting it with a clenched fist, which is tight and contracted from relationship.

Devotion to Avatar Adi Da opens the heart and unlocks the self-contraction. In any moment of true devotional Contemplation of Him, the self-contraction simply dissolves, in the state of Communion with Him—just as the action of opening the hand releases the clench of the fist. As you grow in practice, the habitual activity of self-contraction weakens, and you become more and more deeply established in blissful Communion with Him.

The Four Faculties of the Body-mind

Avatar Adi Da describes four human faculties—the dimensions of the body-mind that "follow the heart" in devotional response to Him:

1. attention (the dimension of mind)
2. feeling (the dimension of emotion)
3. body (the physical dimension)
4. breath (the dimension that connects and unifies the other three faculties).

Ordinarily, the faculties of the body-mind are occupied in various activities, thoughts, and feelings that are the expressions of the self-contraction—the ego's active presumption of being separate from everything and everyone else. When the faculties of attention, feeling, body, and breath turn to Avatar Adi Da, through the attracted heart-response to Him, the self-contraction is instantly undermined. In that moment you are practicing Ruchira Avatara Bhakti Yoga—the concentrated practice (Yoga) of devotion (Bhakti) to the Ruchira Avatar, Adi Da Samraj—thereby enacting the relationship to Him through turning the faculties of the body-mind to Him. In His Words, "you enter My Sphere and leave yours".

Ruchira Avatara Bhakti Yoga is not a form of self-effort or self-manipulation. It is not about intentionally changing the sensations in your body, or the thoughts in your mind, or emotional feelings, or patterns of breathing. Ruchira Avatara Bhakti Yoga is only true when the heart-recognition of the Divine Avatar is alive. Any willful effort to turn the faculties to Him is false devotionalism and not the true Yoga of Ruchira Avatara Bhakti.

Avatar Adi Da describes here the process of surrendering the four faculties to Him:

Instead of wandering in the maze of thoughts, give Me the faculty of mind—which is epitomized by, and as, attention (itself).

Instead of being tossed about by the waves of emotions, give Me the faculty of emotion—which is epitomized by, and as, feeling (itself).

Instead of seeking bodily pleasure and avoiding bodily pain, turn (or face) the body toward My Avatarically-Born bodily (human) Divine Form, and (altogether) give Me the body—through full feeling-intention, enacted through constant devotional service to Me.

The faculties of mind (or attention), emotion (or feeling), and body are connected to one another via the breath—and, thus, the gesture of surrender to Me must also be done via the breath.

Therefore, altogether, in the right and true practice of Ruchira Avatara Bhakti Yoga, mind (or attention), emotion (or feeling), and body are given over to Me, and breathed in heart-Communion with Me.

—Avatar Adi Da Samraj
Da Love-Ananda Gita

There is nothing abstract about this Yoga. It is activated by Avatar Adi Da's Divine Grace when you are directly Contemplating His Incarnation-Body, either through beholding His bodily Form in His physical Presence, or through regarding His photograph, or by simply recollecting His Form in the mind. He Instructs His devotees to wear a locket with a photograph of Him—so that there is no waking moment when one cannot be refreshed in this feeling-Contemplation, and literally turn to His bodily Form.

In the process of this devotion, the "contents" of the faculties are irrelevant. It does not matter how you are feeling at any given moment—which distractions, what wandering in mind, what intense emotions, what bodily discomfort or boredom is being experienced. The liberating truth of Ruchira Avatara Bhakti Yoga is that it is not governed by your experience. It can be practiced in any circumstance, in the "worst" as well as the "best" moment of your life. All you do is turn the faculties at their root, allowing the content to be whatever it is. And you persist in this, even while the content may intensify. In fact, the content will intensify, and it will also be released by the Grace of the Divine Heart-Master, Adi Da. Ruchira Avatara Bhakti Yoga is the great means to transcend the suffering of the self-contraction. Through this practice, the Divine Avatar Works in the body-mind of His devotee, releasing its psycho-physical knots, and establishing a profound equanimity in the being.

Ruchira Avatara Bhakti Yoga Is Eternal

Ruchira Avatara Bhakti Yoga is the essential practice of Adidam from the beginning, and it never ceases. Over time, attention is more and more liberated from bondage to the gross dimension—the world of "money, food, and sex", and social-ego life—and freed up for more and more profound participation in the Spiritual process.

In *The Dawn Horse Testament,* Avatar Adi Da Gives a vivid metaphor for Ruchira Avatara Bhakti Yoga:

Above the clouds, There Is Always The Sun—Forever Free Of Earthly weather. By Tendency, You Are Always Looking At the local weather, and Not At The Sun Itself. That Is What egoity Is About—Always Suffering the changes Of The local Patterning That Is the body-mind In its egoic Bondage. Instead, You Must (In every moment) Turn To Me, Avatarically here-Manifested In Bodily (Human) Divine Form—and You Must Do This Forever, Such That (Ultimately) You Become An egoless Participant In The Conscious Light (or The weatherless Divine and Perfect Sun) Of My Supreme Avataric Divine Gift Of Most Perfect Divine En-Light-enment. . . .

I Am Not "Located" In The Core Of Your Suffering smallness, Below, In The weathering Dark.

The weather (Made By ego) here Can Darken all-and-All—Such That It May Seem To You There Is No Divine (and Perfectly Conscious) Light At All. Nevertheless, In The True Sadhana Of Devotional Turning To Me, There Is No weather—Ever.

This (here) Is "weather-all-the-time"-land. Time is weather. And the body-mind is Always weathered—To the ego's Quick.

Nevertheless, If You Will Live By Always Turning the Total body-mind To My Avatarically-Born Bodily (Human) Divine Form and

Person, You Will (Thus, In Due Course, Progressively and Literally) Incorporate My "Brightness", Making Me The One and Only Condition—Even Of the body-mind and its world.

By Always Turning To My Avatarically-Born Bodily (Human) Divine Form and Person, You Make This (Progressively) By-Me-Avatarically-Given Divine "Brightening" Process Possible—To Begin, and To Go On, and (Ultimately) To Become Perfect.

—Avatar Adi Da Samraj
The Dawn Horse Testament Of The Ruchira Avatar

Ruchira Avatara Bhakti Yoga is summarized in Avatar Adi Da's Admonition, "Invoke Me, Feel Me, Breathe Me, Serve Me", which accounts for each of the four faculties respectively—mind (or attention), emotion (or feeling), breath, and body. Ruchira Avatara Bhakti Yoga is the means to Invoke His "Bright" Presence constantly at the heart. It is the "lifeline" that Avatar Adi Da Gives to His devotee in the midst of this bewildering and mortal existence.

AVATAR ADI DA SAMRAJ: The basic purpose of the body-mind is Invocation of Me. If it is used otherwise, it contracts upon itself. And so, the whole body-mind, from the heart, must Invoke Me.

You must be able to breathe Me, feel Me—beyond fear, sorrow, anger, all un-love, anxiety, the stress of reaction to the gross physical situation.

This is an immense electronic happening, an appearance, most of the dimensions of which are not even suggested in this experience of the human kind. But the fundamental Unity and Reality can and must be Realized, or else there is no Happiness True and Most Profound but only confinement to the mortal view of suffering.

If you are just thinking maybe there is something bigger, you are still being a morsel of sorrowful meat. It is pitiful and sorrowful. So your life must become Invocation of Me. The body-mind must become Invocation of Me, beyond the self-contraction—faith, beyond the mind.

—February 13, 2000

"Come to Me to Realize Me"

In October of 1988 at His Fijian Hermitage, Adidam Samrajashram (Naitauba), Avatar Adi Da Samraj wrote a most beautiful and profound devotional Text—*Da Love-Ananda Gita*—in response to the devotees on retreat in His Hermitage, and to all His devotees everywhere. In this Text, He Instructs His devotees in the core matter of devotion to Him, pointing out that the turning to Him that is the essence of the practice is not for the sake of anything one can attain for oneself.

. . . Come to Me to Realize Me—and do not run from Me after tasting the ordinary meal of conditional knowledge and experience (like a dog runs from its master with a bone).

Having Come to Me, do not look within your body or your mind to discover whether you have received some "thing" from Me (to satisfy your little pouch of separateness).

Rather, surrender and release your <u>total</u> separate (or self-contracted, self-contracting, separative, and always seeking) psycho-physical self (including your entire body, your breath, your emotions, your mind, your knowledge, and all your experiences) by the progressively established and progressively developed Means of devotionally to-Me-Resorting, searchlessly Me-Beholding, receptively to-Me-responding, and (Thus, responsively) ego-surrendering, ego-forgetting, ego-transcending, and (altogether) <u>total</u> psycho-physical feeling-Communion with <u>Me</u>—and, Thus . . . Grow to Luxuriate in My Divine "Bright" Spherical Self-Domain of Love-Bliss.

If you truly and really surrender and release your ego-"I" (or total separate and separative psycho-physical self) to Me—then not any meal of "things" (or effects), but <u>Only</u> I Am the Gift, the Object, the State, and the Realization.

Therefore, Come to Me (and for <u>Me</u> Only), "Bond" to Me (and to <u>Me</u> Only), and Stay with Me (and with <u>Me</u> Only, forever)—and you will (by This) Realize <u>Me</u> (truly, really, and Only).

—Avatar Adi Da Samraj
Da Love-Ananda Gita

Real devotion to Avatar Adi Da is free of any egoic strategy or search. It is love-surrender, made from the heart's own depth—an impulse born of a deep and passionate longing to Realize Him. It is the recognition of Him as one's only true Refuge and Happiness in the midst of all the changes of experience. This is the First Fundamental of the True World-Religion of Adidam. ■

Ruchira Avatara Gita

(The Avataric Way Of The Divine Heart-Master)

by Avatar Adi Da Samraj

This excerpt comprises the first 32 verses—out of 108—of the Ruchira Avatara Gita, *Avatar Adi Da's exposition of the secret of heart-awakened devotion to Him.*

1.

The human voices all call out to the Heart and Person of Real God—Who Lives and Breathes and Feels and Is them, here and now, beyond the ego-"I" and all its search-for-God Ideas:

Heart of hearts, Reveal to us the Truth, the "Bright" Power That Liberates the ego-"I" from itself.

2.

Let us listen and hear the Word Which, when truly Understood, Frees the heart from seeking and un-Happiness. Let us see That Which, when fully Realized, Is the Fullness of Transcendental, Inherently Spiritual, Inherently egoless, and Self-Evidently Divine Being.

3.

Let us Awaken to That Which Is Eternal, and not limited by birth and death. Be Pleased to Reveal to us That Which Is the Supreme Truth.

4.

Heart of hearts, we are desirous of hearing That. Therefore, Sing us the Heart-Word of the Divine Heart-Master, wherein the Divine Heart-Secret is Confessed.

5.

Now, by Heart-Response to the universe of calling prayers, the Living One Breathes them In, and (by This Heart-Song of "Brightest" Words) Out-Breathes the Thunderous Sound That Speaks Love-Bliss to every heart:

Listen to Me with free attention. I will Reveal to you the Heart-Secret of the Divine Heart-Master, Adi Da Samraj—Who Is the Divine World-Teacher Promised for the "late-time", and Who Is the Ruchira Avatar, the Da Avatar, the Love-Ananda Avatar, the First, the Complete, the Last, and the Only Avataric Incarnation of Eleutherios, the Divine Liberator, the "Bright" Divine Heart Itself. His Avataric Divine Self-Confession and His "Bright" Avataric Divine Blessings Destroy all the ills of un-Enlightenment.

6.

The Ruchira Avatar, Adi Da Samraj, Is the First, the Complete, the Last, and the Only Divine Heart-Master. His Principal Divine Names are "Da" (the "Divine Giver", the "First and Original Person", the "Source-Person", the "One and Only Self-Condition of all-and-All"), and "Adi Da" (the "First Giver", the "Original Giver", the "Giving Source", the "Divine Giver of the Divine 'All' to all-and-All"), and "Adi Da Samraj" (the "Self-Giving and All-Giving and to-all-Giving Divine Master of the world", the "One and Only Divine Heart-Master of all-and-All"). And He Is All-"Brightness", Freely Manifesting the Heart's Love-Bliss to all-and-All.

7.

So it was, There, in the Sphere and Sanctuary of His Most Beautiful "Bright" Person—Avatarically Descended in Man-Form to a Place and Motion of His Own, having Said and Made an Earthly Hermitage of His Single Indivisibility, the Man Whose Whitest "Brightness" is, by Means of the Mandalic Prism of our Cosmic Shape, Appearing in His

Own and sudden-colored Summary, Himself a Garden of Luminous Identity, Universally Adorned with Unity and Strength and Love, Roving and Speaking in the manner of all the flowers—the Avatarically Self-Incarnate Divine Person, the Divine and Truly Human Heart-Master, Adi Da Samraj, Thoroughly and Finally Expounded All the Divine and Spiritual Truth of the One Reality to the Great Occasion of His first gathering of devotees. At Last, His Whitest Silence Fell to a Round, like a Breath of True Water, Pressured from Above. One who loved the Master most was sitting close to Him in the Divine Light-Fall, when, in That Sudden of His Avataric Self-"Emergence", her face—like His Own—became translucently "Bright". As she was Merely Beholding Him, in ecstatic love—forgetting herself in the all-at-once of true love's devotional Contemplation of Him—the Divine Self-"Brightness" of Adi Da Samraj Filled (and Over-Filled) her heart, and His Eternal Love-Bliss-Radiance Un-Fractured the Whole of every living part of her. By (Thus) truly Finding Him, the woman (in the Sudden) Realized—beyond all doubt—that she was hearing (and understanding) the True Divine Word, without a thought, and seeing the True Divine Form, even with her own eyes, and recognizing the True Divine Person, with her very heart, and Truly Knowing the One and Spiritual Divine Reality, by Grace of "Brightest" Gift of Only God.

8.

This Gracefully heart-Awakened devotee said out loud, and from her heart, for even all to hear: "Divine Heart-Master, Adi Da Samraj, 'Bright' Before me, I Surrender. You Are the Divine Heart-Master of the entire world. You Are Supreme. You Radiate the 'Bright' Realization of the Supreme. All beings should always heart-recognize You and worship You with true devotion.

9.

You Are the One—the Supreme Being, the Source and Domain of all true worship and right praise.

10.

Radiant Heart, Domain of Truth, please Sing to us the Great Secret of devotion to You, the Divine Heart-Master.

11.

Reveal to us the Secret Method whereby living beings may Realize You, the Transcendental and 'Bright' world-Outshining Real God. I bow down to You, the True and Spiritual and Self-Evidently Divine Person. I worship Your Feet. Kindly Teach the Way of You to all of us."

12.

When the Divine Heart-Master, Adi Da Samraj, Saw this "Bright" face of Awakened devotion and Heard this confession of Great Sight, He Spoke the following Words, His Heart Overflowing with His All-Outshining Joy:

13.

"This is the Secret of all secrets. I could not Speak This Me-Revealing Word until one of you first confessed you see the Vision of Real God in My Avatarically-Born Bodily (Human) Divine Form. I shall Tell you This now, because of your true heart-recognition of Me and your Greatly Awakened devotion to Me.

14.

My Beloved, every one and all—you are each arising in the One 'Bright' Divine Being. This request of yours, made by one who heart-recognizes Me, will benefit all of you, and even the entire world. Therefore, I shall Reveal the Truth and the Way of This Vision to you, for the Sake of all-and-All.

15.

To each one who (by Means of heart-wounded reaching beyond separate and separative self) is truly devoted to the Ever-Living Reality, Truth, and Real God (Which Is Always Already The Case), and who (by Means of My Avataric Divine and heart-Awakening Grace) is truly devoted to Me (heart-recognizing and heart-confessing Me to Be the Very One That Is the One and Only and Self-Evidently Divine Reality and Truth)—My Avatarically-Born Bodily (Human) Divine Form, My Avatarically Self-Transmitted Spiritual (and Always Blessing) Divine Presence, and My Avatarically Self-Revealed (and Very, and Transcendental, and Perfectly Subjective, and Inherently Spiritual, and Inherently egoless, and Inherently Perfect, and Self-Evidently Divine) State are Revealed to Be the Revelation of Real God, the Self-Evidently Divine Person, Manifesting here (and every where in the cosmic domain) As the Divine Heart-Master of all-and-All.

16.

Thus, by Means of true devotional recognition of Me in My here-Born Bodily (Human) Form, I am Found to Be the Avataric Incarnation of the Divine and Only Person. The Truth of devotional recognition of an Avataric Incarnation is Declared by even all the esoteric Scriptures, and even all the esoteric Scriptures Promise the Consummate Avataric Divine Incarnation will Appear in the 'late-time'. So It has been Proven to this Me-seeing devotee—and So do I Affirm the Divine Truth of Me to all of you, and to all-and-All.

17.

I Declare and Affirm the Divine Truth of This Me-Vision, Given to this one by Means of My Avataric Divine Spiritual Grace, and That I would Give to all-and-All. Aham Da Asmi. Beloved, I Am Da, the One and Only One Who Is.

And I Am the First, the Last, and the Only Divine Heart-Master, the Avataric Divine Incarnation every-where-Promised for the 'late-time'. Therefore, listen to My Words and Understand.

18.

The separate traditions of the Great Tradition of religion and Spiritual instruction are often made of false theories, expressed in the words of un-Enlightened beings. Therefore, the multiplication of conventional 'God'-Ideas, ego-serving 'God'-Myths, and partial (or conditional) 'Truths' has confused mankind—but the Divine Heart-Master Comes to Liberate mankind from all confusion of mind, by Avatarically Self-Revealing the Only True and Real God (Who Is Truth Itself, and Reality Itself, and Who Is That Which Is Always Already The Case, beyond the ego-'I').

19.

Prayer, meditation, discipline, philosophy, service—all these are to be built upon the devotional recognition-response to That Which is Revealed In and As the Very Person of the Divine Heart-Master.

20.

Those who are devoted to the Divine Heart-Master hear and see and Realize the Great One As the Divine Heart-Master's Avatarically-Born Bodily (Human) Divine Form, and As His Avatarically Self-Transmitted Divine Body of Spiritual (and Always Blessing) Divine Presence, and As His Avatarically Self-Revealed (and Very, and Transcendental, and Perfectly Subjective, and Inherently Spiritual, and Inherently egoless, and Inherently Perfect, and Self-Evidently Divine) State. Such devotees Declare there is no 'Difference' (and no distinction to be made or acknowledged) between the Divine Heart-Master and the Self-Existing and Self-Radiant Transcendental, Inherently Spiritual, Inherently egoless, and Self-Evidently Divine Being.

21.

Even from the ancient days, many Divinely Gifted sects Proclaim devotion to a genuine (and egoless) Master, saying: 'The Way is to surrender to the Human Master as the Great Person, Divine and Present!' Therefore, look and see in Me the Proof of This Proclamation. I Am the Divine Master of your heart. And if you surrender to Me, I will Confess and Reveal Only Real God to you.

22.

Therefore, those who hear My Avataric Divine Self-Confession and see My Avataric Divine Bodily Self-Revelation must, by Means of their feeling-Contemplation of Me, transcend themselves in Me—the Universally Extended Divine Spiritual Body and Eternal Divine Spirit-Presence That Is Real God, the One and Only and Non-Separate and Indivisible and Inherently egoless Conscious Light That Is the Very Person (or Transcendental Self-Condition) of Real God, and the Self-Existing and Self-Radiant Divine 'Bright' Spherical Self-Domain That Is Real God.

23.

There is no Substitute for Real God.

24.

There is no Substitute for the direct Realization of Real God.

25.

There is no Substitute for your own self-sacrifice in Real God.

26.

The Divine Heart-Master has Realized Real God Most Perfectly, non-separately, beyond relatedness and 'difference'. Therefore, devotees see Real God Revealed In and As and By Means of the Avatarically-Born Bodily (Human) Divine Form of the Divine Heart-Master.

27.

To all those who have This Vision, I Declare:

Aham Da Asmi. Beloved, I Am Da. I Am the Avataric Divine Realizer, the Avataric Divine Revealer, the Avataric Divine Self-Revelation, and the Very (and Self-Evidently Divine) Person of the 'Bright' and Only One. I Am the Demonstration and the Proof of Real God to My devotees. All My devotees are in Me. Therefore, see This Vision, go the Way I will Show to you, and Realize Me.

28.

Do not practice the 'childish cult' of superficial and ego-serving emotionalism (full of wanting dependency, and empty of faith), and do not practice the 'adolescent cult' of non-feeling (willful, self-absorbed, abstract, and independent)—but always practice (and cultivate) the true (and truly feeling, and truly ego-surrendering, and truly ego-forgetting, and truly ego-transcending) Avataric Way of devotion to Me, by Means of right, true, full, and fully devotional (and, in due course, fully Spiritual) practice of the only-by-Me Revealed and Given Way of Adidam (Which is the One and Only by-Me-Revealed and by-Me-Given Way of the Heart).

29.

Neither Real God nor the Divine Heart-Master is your Parent. Therefore, do not expect Real God or the Divine Heart-Master to justify or protect or preserve or fulfill your egoic want and separateness.

30.

You are Called, by Me, to surrender your separate and separative self in Real God. Therefore, cultivate right, true, full, and fully ego-surrendering and ego-forgetting devotion to Me, the Divine Heart-Master—in order to transcend the ego-'I' in My 'Bright' Divine Self-Condition of Being (Itself), Which Is the One and Only Source (and Truth, or Source-Condition) of all-and-All.

31.

To worship the Divine Heart-Master childishly is to worship and serve your separate and separative (or self-contracting) self. To deny or resist the Divine Heart-Master is to worship and serve your separate and separative (or self-contracting) self, adolescently. The separate and separative self (or self-contraction) is, itself and always, the forgetting of the Heart-Source of the world. Therefore, be very and truly devoted to Me, the Divine Master of your heart—but not for the sake of ego-salvation, or the glorification of your separate and separative self. Worship Me by surrendering your ego-'I' to Me. Surrender to Me in order to forget and transcend your separate and separative self in Me. Forget and transcend your ego-'I' in Me, in order that you may (by Means of My Avataric Divine Spiritual Grace) Remember and Realize Me, the Divine Person and Heart-Source of all-and-All.

32.

I Am the Sign and the Revelation and the Proof of Real God in the world. I Am the Testament and the Means of Freedom Itself. I Am Eleutherios, the Divine Liberator, Who Is Freedom Itself."

SECOND FUNDAMENTAL

A New Pattern of Life

Supporting the Practice of Devotion with Form and Discipline

The practice of the . . . Way of Adidam is founded in the transcending of the human psycho-physical structure—but not by means of a dissociative act. Thus, the fundamental (and necessary) basis for the practice of the . . . Way of Adidam . . . is equanimity relative to one's own psycho-physical structure and relative to the psycho-physical context of human (and cosmic) existence.

—Avatar Adi Da Samraj
Real God Is The Indivisible Oneness Of Unbroken Light

In the first sixty years of His Life, Avatar Adi Da undertook a thorough investigation of all aspects of human life for the sake of Revealing the complete Way of Divine Realization, the true world-religion that can be embraced by any and all. He left no part of human existence untouched by His Divine Wisdom. A fundamental lesson emerged from that investigation: The ego is programmed, or patterned, to seek its own satisfaction, under any and all circumstances—whether in the ordinary dimensions of life or even in religious and Spiritual terms. Thus, if our lives are not re-patterned—such that we go beyond the orientation to self-fulfillment—our being is literally shut off from the Divine.

During His Teaching years, Avatar Adi Da also Revealed that the true Spiritual process cannot take place unless the body-mind enjoys the equanimity of being rightly oriented to the Divine. The body-mind is not "automatically" ready for Spiritual life—there is preparation that must take place in order to be capable of receiving Avatar Adi Da's Spiritual Transmission. This preparation requires that all four faculties be consistently turned to Him, such that the being is granted freedom from the ego-programs of separateness.

The Spiritual process in the Way of Adidam is about "Enlightenment of the whole body". By contrast, the ego is the contraction of the whole body. Ego-transcending devotion to Avatar Adi Da, turning the faculties of the body-mind to Him, must be lived concretely and demonstrated in every area of life. It is thus that the being transcends the impulse to self-fulfillment in body and mind. And it is for this reason that disciplines are introduced into the life of devotional turning to Avatar Adi Da—in order to support the deepening of that process.

Life-Discipline Is an Aid to Transcending the Limiting Structures of the Human Body-Mind

Avatar Adi Da describes three fundamental dimensions of human experience:

1. gross
2. subtle
3. causal

The gross (or outer) dimension corresponds to the physical level of experience and the waking state.

The subtle (or inner) dimension includes the dimension of the life-energy and also everything to do with mind—both the conceptual mind and the domain of dreaming and psychic experience, including the range of supernormal experience that is commonly called "mystical".

The causal (or root) dimension refers to the depth where the "root" (or "causative") act of attention occurs in Consciousness—giving rise to the sense of the dichotomy between "I" and "other". This original (and always constant) act of separation is the root-form of the self-contraction, and (therefore) the root of human suffering.

Avatar Adi Da has also Revealed how the being tends to interpret reality (and any perception) according to its own point of view, or "level" of vision. We are literally "trapped" in interpretations of reality and experience, based on our own limited views. For example, those bound to the gross dimension of experience tend to interpret reality to be merely physical—and composed of discrete, separate entities. In contrast, the process and progress of the Way of Adidam is founded in an understanding of the Indivisible Unity that is prior to any experience, knowledge, or separate consciousness.

No level of the human structure is, in and of itself, Spiritual or Divine. Thus, none of the structures of the body-mind is the means or method of transformation in the Way of Adidam. Rather, the entire being is devotionally turned (and, thereby, surrendered) to Avatar Adi Da. This devotional turning allows the being to outgrow all points of view, progressively, by His Divine Spiritual Grace. His Spiritual Transmission is the "Bright" Itself, Beyond all the structures of the self-contracted body-mind—gross, subtle, and causal.

The life-disciplines of Adidam are a means of turning the faculties of the body-mind to Him particularly in the context of the gross dimension (or the world of "money, food, and sex" and social egoity). By means of Avatar Adi Da's Divine Grace, and via embrace of all of the fundamentals of the Way of Adidam, all limits—at every level of the being—are progressively purified and transformed. It is thus that the gross, subtle, and causal aspects of the being cease to obstruct and limit the reception of His Spiritual Transmission and (most ultimately) the Awakening to His "Bright" Divine Condition.

Life-Positive Discipline

Avatar Adi Da has established a complete range of disciplines relative to functional and practical life for His devotees. These disciplines are established at the very beginning of the practice of Adidam, and you maintain the basic design of life-discipline (continuing to refine it) from that point on.

The disciplines of the Way of Adidam are "life-positive" because they are based in the disposition of accepting the realities of human life (such as the basic matters of "money, food, and sex"), rather than making any kind of attempt to "get away" (or "escape") from these realities. The disciplines bring equanimity and well-being to the entire being—body, emotion, mind, and breath. (Detailed instruction in all of the principles and practices described here is given in the literature and coursework published by the Avataric Pan-Communion of Adidam.)

Even more, the disciplines are "life-positive" because (as Avatar Adi Da describes) they are a means to "allow the body-mind to become a participant in the Divine Spiritual Sphere of Existence". Thus, the aim of the life-disciplines in the Way of Adidam is not a merely moralistic or puritanical attempt to be "well behaved" (in the manner of conventional religion), nor is it a means of intentionally dissociating from the body-mind (in the manner of traditional ascetic practice). The purpose of the life-disciplines of Adidam is entirely a matter of allowing your body-mind to become an ever greater "vessel" for receiving Avatar Adi Da's Spiritual Transmission of the "Bright". And when the body-mind is infused by His Divine Transmission, further transformation occurs in the body, mind, psyche, and relations—without any effort on your part.

AVATAR ADI DA SAMRAJ: There is a traditional notion that the way to Realize the Divine Condition is to excise or shut down or eliminate the body-mind in some strategic effort. What I have Proven, Demonstrated, and Taught you is that such is not the true method. Such strategic effort is the method of egoity itself, and only becomes more so. The Way of Adidam is not about strategic dissociation from the body-mind as a technique, but (rather) surrender <u>as</u> the

Avatar Adi Da has established a complete range of disciplines relative to functional and practical life for His devotees.

body-mind. The Way of Adidam is utter surrender of the body-mind—transcending it by surrendering as it, rather than trying to dissociate from it.

This is a very practical matter, then. The method of egoity is dissociative. The Means of Divine Self-Realization is the relationship to Me, whole bodily turning to Me. It is surrender as the body-mind, turning the faculties to Me, entering into Communion with Me on the basis of surrender as the body-mind. On that basis, I am Able to Do My Blessing-Work of Transmission of the "Bright", Transmission of the Divine Self-Condition. In the surrendered disposition, My devotee becomes combined with My Spiritually Self-Transmitted Person.

—March 15, 2003

A Story of Avatar Adi Da's Instruction: The Life-Disciplines Must Serve the Spiritual Process— Not Merely the Psychic Processes Potential for Human Beings

One of the matters of ongoing debate relative to the life-disciplines appropriate for Spiritual practitioners is the usefulness of intoxicants. Can there be a Spiritual usefulness in the mild intoxication that results from tobacco, for example? Or in the intoxication brought on by alcohol? Or (in the Pacific island cultures) in the calming and slightly narcotic intoxication of kava?

During the years of Avatar Adi Da's Teaching-Work, there were occasions when these substances were used, as part of His in-life "consideration" of the God-Realizing process and right discipline in the context of it. When that 30-year "consideration" was finally complete, Avatar Adi Da made clear that, in the process of Divine Realization, the appropriate discipline relative to intoxicants is not to use them at all.*

Why He says this is explained in a story about a Fijian devotee.

Solomone Finau (or "Solo") has always had a deep devotional response to Avatar Adi Da, since he first saw Avatar Adi Da in 1983. In October 2002, Solo was serving Avatar Adi Da at His Hawaiian Hermitage Ashram, Da Love-Ananda Mahal. As a Fijian who was brought up in the traditional way, Solo has a real respect and appreciation for the serious purpose of the traditional kava ceremony in Fiji, which was originally used as a means of contacting ancestral spirits. Solo was also aware that kava had been sacredly used at one time in traditional Hawaiian culture, and he asked Avatar Adi Da if it would be appropriate to perform the traditional kava ceremony at Da Love-Ananda Mahal, as a way of making positive contact with the local Hawaiian spirits. The Instruction that Avatar Adi Da Gave in response to Solo's question is characteristic

*Avatar Adi Da allows, however, that there may be sacred social occasions in which it is appropriate to make token (or symbolic) use of one of the socially common intoxicants (alcohol, tobacco, or kava) for the purpose of respectful participation in the occasion.

of the profound "consideration" that Avatar Adi Da has engaged relative to the optimum forms of life-discipline.

In this Communication, Avatar Adi Da draws a distinction between the psychic process (of stimulating the dreaming mind, becoming aware of the archetypal world of the unconscious, contacting the spirit-worlds, and so on) and the true Spiritual process (of receiving the tangible and life-transforming Spiritual Transmission of a Transmission-Master). And He also clarifies the true purpose of life-discipline in the Way of Adidam.

AVATAR ADI DA SAMRAJ: Most indigenous cultures around the world have some substance or other that they use as a means of stimulating the brain-mind to produce psychic content—used in a formalized manner, often ritually, and so on. In Fiji (and other island cultures of the Pacific), the traditional substance is kava. In the "Westernized" world, alcohol is the substance used to produce psychological and psychic brain-mind phenomena. Tobacco is another substance that has been used in this magic-based manner in shamanistic cultures.

The use of such substances is about stimulating the psyche—but the psyche is not (itself) the vehicle of Spiritual life. And when these substances that are traditionally used in a sacred manner to stimulate the psyche come to be used socially for their own sake (to stimulate psychological or emotional effects), then they become even rather degrading and degenerative, causing both health problems and social problems.

In any case, these various naturally occurring substances produce a kind of hallucinogenic or psyche-stimulating or brain-mind-stimulating effect. The traditional use of these substances is part of the vitally-based and psyche-based cultural order of traditional societies—a cultural order that is not (itself) in the domain of Spirituality. The real Spiritual process is quite a different thing than the psyche-based magical (or shamanistic) process cultivated in such societies.

The stimulation of the psyche for its own purposes is not (in and of itself) a Spiritual process. Therefore, the use of traditional intoxicating substances—whether in the social manner (which is basically just degenerative or just an occasional social amusement) or in the ritual manner presumed to be sacred (in order to produce psychic effects)—is not useful Spiritually. In fact, it is basically counterproductive, because it creates a habit-orientation in the body-mind that is (on the one hand) grossly self-indulgent, degenerative, and ego-possessed, and (on the other hand) involved in the domain of brain-mind and psyche. Such involvement in the domain of the brain-mind and the psyche does not allow the body-mind to become a participant in the all-Transcending (and, therefore, psyche-Transcending) Divine Spiritual Sphere of Existence. Thus, such involvement is an obstruction to the Spiritual process.

In the Way of Adidam, the psyche is transcended in the real Spiritual process. It is not made into a thing in itself, to be stimulated for its own sake. Rather, the psyche is made a participant in the Divine Spiritual Self-Condition by transcending itself in devotional and Spiritual Communion with Me. So the entire body-mind in its totality (including the psyche) is surrendered into a participatory involvement in My Person and (therefore) in the Spiritual Process and the Divine Self-Condition. Therefore, My devotees must rightly discipline the body-mind, in order to keep it free of encumbrances that work against the Spiritual process.

All of My Instruction relative to life-disciplines comes from this basis. Therefore, the life-disciplines are not about purity for its own sake, nor are they about some kind of moralistic conventions of social behavior. Thus, one should be firm and intelligent about the disciplines, but not self-righteous, moralistic, or puritanical.

When the real ego-transcending Spiritual process is understood and really engaged, then there emerges a clear understanding of the kind of limitations that people build into the body and the psyche—limitations that encumber or prevent the Spiritual process. There are many habits and patterns of the body-mind—physical, psychological, psychic, and so on—which must be relinquished in the practice of Adidam. Such relinquishing is never to be undertaken for moralistic or puritanical reasons. Rather, such relinquishing is entirely based on the understanding of life as an ego-transcending process of total psycho-physical surrender into the Divine Spiritual Self-Condition.

—October 7, 2002

The Simple Intelligence of Right Diet

The gross body is, very simply, the food-body. The gross body (itself) depends on (and is made of) food. The quality and quantity of food largely (or very basically) determines the state and desire and action of the physical body and the sense-mind. If food-taking is intelligently minimized, and if the food selected is both pure and purifying, then the physical body (and even the entire emotional dimension of the being, and the total mind) passes through a spontaneous natural cycle that shows (progressive) signs of (first) purification, (then) rebalancing, and (finally) rejuvenation. . . . Therefore, primarily, it is through the food-discipline (accompanied by general self-discipline) that gross bodily purification, rebalancing, and rejuvenation are accomplished.

—Avatar Adi Da Samraj
Santosha Adidam

Avatar Adi Da points out that one of the most basic ways to keep the faculties of the body-mind available to be turned to Him is via the discipline of what we eat. The basic discipline relative to food in the Way of Adidam involves purification, rebalancing, and rejuvenation of the physical body through an optimum personal diet and periodic fasting.

In the face of all the confusing and contradictory alternatives championed in the world of health and nutrition, Avatar Adi Da's Instruction is simply a sane and rational approach to discovering the optimum dietary practice in the context of a life of Communion with Him:

The right and optimum diet is (necessarily) a conservative diet. In right (or effective) practice of the Way of Adidam, dietary discipline fully serves the submission of personal energy and attention to the Great Process that becomes Most Perfect Divine Self-Realization. Therefore, the right and optimum diet must be intelligently moderated in its quantity and carefully selected in its quality, so that it will not burden the physical body or bind the mind (or attention) through food-desire and negative (or constipating, toxifying, and enervating) food-effects (and ingestion-effects in general), and so that (along with the necessary additional "consideration" and really effective transcending of aberrated, anxious, or even excessively private habits and patterns relative to food-taking and waste elimination) it serves the yielding of free human energy and attention to the great (and, necessarily, Devotional) process (of self-surrender, self-forgetting, progressive self-observation, eventual most fundamental self-understanding, and, altogether, more and more effective self-transcendence, or ego-transcendence) that is the necessary foundation of the Way of Adidam. Consequently, right and optimum diet must (to the maximum degree that is both right and possible) be natural, fresh, whole, wholesome, balanced, balancing, pure (or non-toxic), and purifying—or, in the language of tradition, "sattvic". And right and optimum diet must (to the maximum degree that is both right and possible) be limited to what is necessary and sufficient for bodily (and general psycho-physical) purification, balance, well-being, and appropriate service.

—Avatar Adi Da Samraj
Santosha Adidam

In the Way of Adidam, by following the guidelines given in Avatar Adi Da's Teaching, you discover and adapt to the diet that supports devotional Communion with Him—because it frees energy and attention for the devotional and Spiritual process in His Company. (This adaptation is made in consultation with medical professionals and devotees who are trained to assist in the process.) For most people, the optimum diet is a vegetarian diet that includes a significant proportion of raw foods—offering the body the maximum life-force and nutrition, without burdening the body with unnecessary toxicity that leads to enervation and disease.

Right Practice in the Realm of Sex and Emotion

Since the beginning of His Teaching-Work, Avatar Adi Da has made clear that the Spiritual process requires a straightforward and thorough address to the dimension of sexuality. This is the case whether or not an individual chooses a sexually active life.

Avatar Adi Da has always approached sexuality and its attendant emotions as a single area of "consideration". To clearly indicate the interconnectedness of emotion and sex, He speaks of the "emotional-sexual" aspect of life. And He has always addressed the emotional-sexual matter with complete freedom, entirely without suppression or moralistic attitudes—something completely unique in the annals of religious and Spiritual Teaching. The emotional-sexual disciplines that He offers are given entirely from the point of view of what is required for the true Spiritual process to fulfill itself in His Company.

As Avatar Adi Da makes clear, the sex function (in and of itself) is not a "problem". Rather, it is the bondage to the search for emotional-sexual self-fulfillment (whether or not one is sexually active) that is a principal obstruction to the process of true religion and Real-God-Realization. Avatar Adi Da acknowledges the accuracy of Sigmund Freud's basic observation that every human being is deeply affected by his or her infantile experience—particularly the relationships to mother and father. Avatar Adi Da points out that every individual, based on early-life experiences in relation to his or her parents, exhibits particular (deeply patterned) emotional-sexual characteristics. The emotional-sexual character and its pattern of seeking for fulfillment is revealed not only in the intimate setting with a partner. The pattern is animated all the time—in relationship to all men, to all women, and even to one's own body. Based on this reality, Avatar Adi Da has given His devotees an emotional-sexual practice that encompasses the entire relational dimension of life, as well as a specific sexual Yoga.

In *The Dawn Horse Testament*, the Divine Avatar summarizes the core of His Instruction relative to right relational life:

For those who Are Committed To Love (and who, Therefore, Always Commune With Me, The One Who Is Love-Bliss Itself), Even Rejection By others Is Received and Accepted As A Wound, Not An Insult. Even The Heart-Necessity To Love and To Be Loved Is A Wound. And Even The Fullest Realization Of My Love-Bliss Is A Wound That Never Heals.

The egoic Ritual Calls every individual To Defend himself or herself Against The Wounds Of Love and The Wounding Signs Of Un-Love (or egoic self-Contraction) In the daily world. Therefore, Even In The Context Of "True Yogic Intimacy" . . . , The Tendency (Apart From Spiritual Responsibility) Is To Act As If Every Wound (Which Is Simply A Hurt) Is An Insult (or A Reason To Punish).

In The Only-By-Me Revealed and Given Way Of Adidam, The Reactive Rituals Of egoity Must Be Released By The ego-Transcending (and, In Due Course, Spiritually Activated) Practice Of Devotion To Me. This Requires Each and Every Practitioner Of The Way Of Adidam To Observe, Understand, and Relinquish The emotionally Reactive Cycle Of Rejection and Punishment. And The Necessary Prerequisites For Such Relinquishment Are Vulnerability (or The Ability To Feel The Wounds Of Love Without Retaliation), Sensitivity To the other In Love (or The Ability To Sympathetically Observe, Understand, Forgive, Love, and Not Punish or Dissociate From the other In Love), and Love Itself (or The Ability To Love, To Know You Are Loved, To Receive Love, and To Know That Both You and the other, Regardless Of Any Appearance To The Contrary, Are Vulnerable To Love and Heart-Requiring Of Love).*

It Is Not Necessary (or Even Possible) To Become Immune To The Feeling Of Being Rejected. To Become Thus Immune, You Would Have To Become Immune To Love Itself. What Is Necessary (and Also Possible) Is To Enter Fully (and Fully Devotionally) Into The Spiritual Life-Sphere Of Love. In The Only-By-Me Revealed and Given Way Of Adidam, This Is Done By First Entering (Devotionally, and, Thus, By Heart) Into My Humanly-Incarnated Divine Spiritual Company, and (Therein) Surrendering To My Divine Spiritual "Embrace" Of Love-Bliss—Wherein You Are Not Merely Loved As a self-Contracted

*In *The Dawn Horse Testament Of The Ruchira Avatar*, one of the principal references to the Way of Adidam that Adi Da Samraj uses is "The Way Of The Heart". For the sake of simplicity and clarity in this book, these references have been changed to "The Way Of Adidam".

ego-"I", but You Are (To The Degree That, By Means Of My Avatarically Self-Transmitted Divine Spiritual Grace, the ego-"I" Is Surrendered, Forgotten, and Transcended In Me) Awakened To Be (and To Show) Love-Bliss Itself. Then You Must, Through Life-Active Devotion To Me, Allow The Demonstration Of My Own Love-Bliss-Radiance In the world of Your human relationships.

—Avatar Adi Da Samraj
The Dawn Horse Testament Of The Ruchira Avatar

Thus, a key aspect of right emotional-sexual practice (both for those who are sexually active and for those who are celibate) consists of observing and understanding habitual patterns of un-love. And at the same time, you also begin consciously developing the practice of active love, based in heart-Communion with Avatar Adi Da.

In the practice of Adidam, not only is emotional-sexual life converted to the disposition of love, intimacy, and Communion with Avatar Adi Da, but there is also a specific sexual Yoga (to be engaged by those who are involved in sexually active intimate relationship).

The conventional orgasm, in both men and women, is a degenerative event, in which the energy of the body is actually "thrown out" and thus wasted. Through adaptation to simple practices, you can bypass degenerative orgasm and convert it into a regenerative event, which generates positive flows of hormonal energy. The sexual Yoga involves precisely described practices relative to breathing, to the conducting of both natural energy (and, in due course, Avatar Adi Da's Spirit-Energy) through the body, to bodily "locks" that assist in the bypass of degenerative orgasm and the conversion of degenerative orgasm into regenerative orgasm, to the means for increasing one's ability to allow more intense flows of sexual energy, and so on. For those involved in a sexually active intimate relationship (whether heterosexual or homosexual), this process develops into the practice of deep sexual embrace with your intimate, in the context of devotional and Spiritual heart-Communion with Avatar Adi Da.

The emotional-sexual Yoga of Adidam is not a kind of "tantric" practice that works with the energies of sexuality and "raises them up" so as to move you "toward" Enlightenment.

Contrary To The Illusions Of Certain Forms Of (conventional, or Traditional) Tantrism, No Form Of Cultivating sexual energy Can (In Any Sense) Cause Spiritual Growth. That Is To Say, sexuality Is Not (In Any Sense) Causative Relative To Spirituality. The Illusion That sexuality Can Cause Spiritual Growth Stems From The Fundamental Illusion That Spiritual Practice Is A Process That Starts "Below", and Moves From there To Above. That Illusion Is An Unwitting Validation Of egoity—A Declaration That, In Effect, the ego Must "Propel" itself Upward, To The Divine (Thus, "Taking Heaven By Storm"). Such Is, In Reality, The Exact Opposite Of What Occurs In The Real Spiritual Process In My Avataric Divine Spiritual Company. In That Process, I (The "Bright" Divine Reality, In Avataric Divine Person) Come Down—and I Spiritually In-Fill You.

—Avatar Adi Da Samraj
The Dawn Horse Testament Of The Ruchira Avatar

The process of emotional-sexual practice in Adidam is "sex-transcending" in the sense that the emotional-sexual aspect of the being is re-oriented from the purposes of self-fulfillment to the purpose of ego-transcending Communion with Avatar Adi Da Samraj. In the progress of the Way of Adidam, emotional-sexual practice is more and more conformed to the process of reception of Avatar Adi Da's Spiritual Transmission. As that Spiritual reception becomes the primary process of life, all aspects of ordinary life (including sex) become entirely secondary to the fullness of the devotional and Spiritual Communion with Avatar Adi Da. Thus, you more and more measure all functions of the body-mind by what preserves and cultivates reception of that Divine Transmission.

In *The Dawn Horse Testament*, Avatar Adi Da summarizes His Instruction about emotional-sexual life:

I Have Observed That sex—or, More Accurately, emotional-sexual life—Is The Primary Obsession Of human beings, Especially In The Earlier Stages Of Life. Human beings Are self-Driven To Fulfill their emotional-sexual Motivations—To The Extent That their Urge To emotional-sexual Fulfillment Has The Force Of a philosophy. Their Involvement In emotional-sexual life Is, In Effect, A philosophical Commitment (Expressed At The personal Level) To Find Perfect self-Fulfillment In The Purposes Of ordinary human life.

This emotional-sexual Search Is, Therefore, a kind of utopian philosophy—a philosophy About Being Finally Fulfilled and Perfectly pleasurized In life. But the philosophy Of The emotional-sexual Search Allows human beings To Ignore Both their mortality and The Ultimate (Un-conditional, Indivisible, Divine, and Spiritual) Condition Of Reality Itself. Therefore, that philosophy Is False. Like the philosophy of scientific materialism, the philosophy Of Ultimate emotional-sexual self-Fulfillment Is Based On A Misinterpretation Of Reality, A False Presumption About Reality.

There Are all kinds of conventional social rules For Controlling sexual behavior—but they Are Designed To Serve The Purposes Of the social ego, and (Therefore) Have Nothing To Do With ego-Transcendence or Spiritual Realization. Merely To Become a "well-behaved" social ego Is Not A Sufficient Basis For Entering Into The Real Spiritual Process.

The Great Tradition Of Mankind Is, As A Whole, Unresolved and Ambivalent Relative To The Entire Matter Of sexuality—and It Is Even Generally sex-Negative (or "sex-paranoid") In Its Orientation. All Such puritanical Righteousness Must Be Gone Beyond. Otherwise, one's emotional-sexual egoity Is Never Truly Inspected and Dealt With. In That Case, attention Remains Fundamentally (Even If Unconsciously) Bound In emotional-sexual dilemmas of all kinds, Thereby limiting The Degree Of Real Spiritual Growth That Is Possible.

I Am The One Who Has Completed The Great "Consideration" Of human emotional-sexual life—and I Did So For The Sake Of every one. I Am The One Who Has Made It Possible For human beings To Totally Comprehend The emotional-sexual Dimension Of Existence, and To Completely Transcend egoic Reactivity, and To Truly Grow Beyond the ordinary emotional-sexual limitations that the worldly mind Represents, and (By All Of This) To Have an Altogether—and In Reality—Sane life. Indeed, Such emotional-sexual Clarity and Integrity Is Essential For The Real Spiritual Process.

In The Great Tradition, Various Kinds Of emotional-sexual Discipline Have Been Required or Recommended—but None Of

These Disciplines Were Sufficient For The Thorough Transcending Of The emotional-sexual ego. In The Only-by-Me Revealed and Given Way Of Adidam, the emotional-sexual ego (and, Indeed, the ego of "money, food, and sex" Altogether) Must Be Really and Truly Gone Beyond—and This Must, In Real and Significant Terms, Begin In The Foundation Stage Of Practice Of The Way Of Adidam, As Part Of The (From Thence, Ongoing) Basis For Real and True Growth Into (and In) The By-Me-Spiritually-Initiated (and Always Newly By-Me-Spiritually-Activated) Stages Of The Only-By-Me Revealed and Given Way Of Adidam.

"Consider" This: sex Is Not The "Great Evil". Indeed, sex Is Not Evil At All. Rather, egoity Is The Root and Source Of All Evil and All Problems. I Have Revealed and Demonstrated That sex Is Transformed and Made Right Only Through The Process Of Transcending egoity. Therefore, sex itself Need Not—and Should Not—Be Regarded As an "enemy". It Is emotional-sexual egoity That Must Be Gone Beyond. Thus, What Must Be (Most Fundamentally) Addressed Relative To Your emotional-sexual life Is Not sex In and Of itself, but Your egoic Search For self-Fulfillment By Means Of sex.

While It Is True That sex Is Not The "Great Evil", It Is Equally True That sex Is Not The "Great Salvation". In All The Years Of My Avataric Divine Teaching-Work and My Avataric Divine Revelation-Work (and, Indeed, In My Own "Sadhana Years"), I Thoroughly Demonstrated and Proved That A sexually active Yoga Carries No Advantage (and Is Not Causative) Relative To The Process Of Real-God-Realization. Indeed, The Most That Can Be Accomplished By Means Of A (Necessarily, Profoundly Seriously—and, In General, Very Conservatively—Engaged) sexually active Yoga Is To Make one's emotional-sexual Practice Compatible With The Real Spiritual Process (Whatever That Requires In The individual Case), Such That sexual activity Does Not Actively Obstruct The Spiritual Process. And All Of My Devotees who Grow Into The (Spiritually) Fully Technically Responsible Stages Of The Only-By-Me Revealed and Given Way Of Adidam Will, Whether Sooner Or Later, Be Spontaneously (and Spiritually) Moved To Greatly Conserve (or Even To Entirely Relinquish) sexual activity—For The Very Reason That It Tends To

Work Against The Fullest (and, At Last, Most Perfect) Spiritual Reception and Realization Of Me. . . .

The Only-By-Me Revealed and Given Way Of Adidam Does Not Develop "From Below Upwards". The Notion (or philosophy) Of "From Below Upwards" Is The Root-Error Of The egoic (and Traditional) Spiritual Search, Suggesting That the "dog" Must Be "Washed" From the "tail" Toward the "head".

"Below" Is Not (and Never Can Be) Causative Relative To What Is Above. Rather, What Is Above Must Purify and Transform and (Most Ultimately) En-Light-en What Is "Below".

That Is How I Do My Avataric Divine Spiritual Work.

That Is The Nature Of The Real Spiritual Process In My Avataric Divine Company.

Thus, The Real Spiritual (and Yogic) Process In My Avataric Divine Company Is Not A Development From A sexual Base (or From Any Base That Is "Below"). In Other Words, The Real Reception Of My Avataric Divine Spiritual Self-Transmission Is Not (Itself) A Process Of The Return Of sexual energy (From "Below" To Above), or, Otherwise, Of Negatively (or, Otherwise, egoically) Programming the body-mind Relative To sexual energy (or sexuality itself).

My Avataric Divine Spiritual Self-Transmission Comes From Utterly Above and Beyond—To Pervade and Purify and Transform and Awaken What Is "Below".

Nevertheless, In Order To Receive Me Spiritually (From Above and Beyond), You Must (Surely) Discipline (and Turn To Me—In My Avatarically-Born Bodily Human Divine Form here) All Of What Is "Below" (In emotional-sexual Terms, and In All Other Terms)—By Preparing (and Always Maintaining) Your body-mind For My Freely Given Avataric Divine Spiritual Invasion.

—Avatar Adi Da Samraj
The Dawn Horse Testament Of The Ruchira Avatar

"Conscious Exercise"

The basic disciplines relative to general health in the Way of Adidam involve the practice of what Avatar Adi Da calls "conscious exercise". "Conscious exercise" consists of systematic physical exercises and bodily practices that are combined with feeling-awareness of the breath and the flow of natural life-energy. Avatar Adi Da has given Instruction in the optimum form for sitting, standing, and walking, and He has developed unique programs of calisthenics, hatha yoga, and chi gong (an ancient Chinese energy-practice)—all of which are designed to maximize not only the flow of natural life-energy in the body-mind, but also (in the Spiritually initiated stages of practice of Adidam) the ability to receive and conduct Avatar Adi Da's Divine Spiritual Transmission.

The usual activity of most human beings involves a compulsive breaking and obstructing of the life-current, thus creating tensions and inharmonies within the body. Whether acting or at rest, people are usually involved in an endless ritual of twitching and shifting the body, always compensating for the pain and discomfort of their habitual condition. However, through the conscious use of the body, while being randomly mindful of bodily movement and posture and while performing "conscious exercise", one is able to observe and understand the ritual of bodily compensations and pass beyond them into a stable, harmonious condition wherein attention and energy are free for devotional service. Therefore, as My devotee, learn to use the whole body consciously, both in ordinary life and in meditation.

—Avatar Adi Da Samraj
Conscious Exercise and the Transcendental Sun

Service

In the Way of Adidam, the basic practice of service involves a reorientation of life—work, money, and even all activities—from the ego-serving disposition to the disposition of cooperation and service to others. Principally, this is done by living in devotional service to Avatar Adi Da and His Divine Work in the world.

In *The Dawn Horse Testament*, Avatar Adi Da gives this description of the basic discipline of service:

In The Only-By-Me Revealed and Given Way Of Adidam, The Basic Disciplines Relative To Service Involve The Transcending Of the social ego, By Means Of The Re-Orientation Of social activity, work, money, and, Indeed, Even all activities, To The ego-Transcending, Cooperative, Inclusive, and other-Serving Disposition, and (Altogether) To An Intention That Is, Characteristically (and Always Positively, Rather Than Insipidly), Harmless (or Inspired To Love), and, Characteristically, Both Pro-Relational and Positively Relational (and, Therefore, Not Fundamentally Separative and Competitive, but Positively Alive, Without Negative, or Loveless, Intentions—and Actively Competitive, or Even Rightly Aggressive, Only By Necessity, In circumstances that Either Strictly Demand Or Rightly Expect Competitiveness, or Even, At times, ego-Transcending Aggressiveness). And, In The Process Of This Re-Orientation, There Must Also Be The Effective Relinquishment Of The ego-Serving, Separative (or Exclusive), ego-Fulfilling, Basically Competitive, and (Otherwise) Negative (or Loveless, and, Characteristically, Not Positively Harmless, Not Love-Inspired, and Not all-and-All-Including) Disposition. And All Of This Is To Be Accomplished Simply By Engaging all activities (functional, practical, relational, and Cultural) As . . . ego-Surrendering, ego-Forgetting, More and More ego-Transcending, and Always Directly and Really Felt Devotional, and Truly Me-Contemplating, Service To Me—As An Extension Of My Devotee's Practice Of Ruchira Avatara Bhakti Yoga Into Every Kind and Form Of his or her Active Participation In human life.

—Avatar Adi Da Samraj
The Dawn Horse Testament Of The Ruchira Avatar

Money as Energy

The disposition of service in the Way of Adidam also includes a cooperative and sacred orientation to the use of money. Devotees of Avatar Adi Da understand money as a tangible representation of life-energy—and choose to maximize the commitment of life-energy to the sacred purposes of Avatar Adi Da's Spiritual Blessing-Work and the communication of the Way of Adidam. Avatar Adi Da describes the principles underlying the practice of tithing (and financial integrity altogether):

AVATAR ADI DA SAMRAJ: Tithing is the traditional financial gesture of a religious practitioner. The principle of tithing, and of any form of regular financial support, is that one gives a portion of one's goods to the Divine for the Sake of the Divine. Such a gift is given without expectations. One gives to the Divine because the Divine Is the Divine, and because the Divine has Purposes that must be served—not only by the right use of money, but by all the forms of human energy. The tithe is not the same as the dues paid by a club member. Nor is it a payment in expectation for services. A tithe is a gift to the Divine.

Money Is Simply a Sign of Human Energy

Right involvement with (and right management of) money is part of the responsibility you must assume for your own life (both in the personal context and in the collective context) when you become My formally practicing devotee. Thus, for My devotee, money (and food, and sex) must become an expression of the total commitment of life's energy and activity to counter-egoic effort and ego-transcending love. . . .

It has traditionally been said that money is "the root of all evil". However, this traditional saying does not mean that money itself is evil. In and of itself, money is neither positive nor negative. Money is simply a sign of human energy. Money is made into a positive or negative sign depending on one's disposition toward it and toward life altogether. Therefore, if you are My devotee, the necessary and inevitable involvement with money is something to be made right, something to be transformed—not something to be merely eschewed (or, otherwise, merely wasted). . . .

If you are My devotee, you must make money into an expression of the fullness of your devotional energy and your ego-transcending disposition altogether, including your disposition toward the life-pattern of real and true cooperation.

—Avatar Adi Da Samraj
Santosha Adidam

Cooperative Sacred Culture

The life-disciplines relative to diet, sexuality, "conscious exercise", and service are practiced in the context of the sacred culture of other formal practitioners of Adidam. That worldwide sacred culture constitutes a "global ashram", and it gives Spiritual practice a context of both inspiration and expectation, as well as a supportive setting for devotion to Avatar Adi Da and ego-transcending cooperation.

While it is optimal for practitioners of Adidam to live in proximity to a regional community of other practitioners (so that you can maximize participation in the cooperative culture of Adidam), it is also entirely possible to participate in the "global ashram" from anywhere in the world. You do this by maximizing your participation with other practitioners through regular, accountable affiliation with your nearest regional center and through participation in the online cooperative culture via the internet.

Adidam has regional communities throughout the world, and centers in the United States, Canada, Great Britain, the Netherlands, Germany, Australia, New Zealand, and Fiji, with bookstores, public centers, and formal meditation halls. Other cooperative services are offered to devotees through the cooperative community organizations of Adidam—including the Radiant Life Cultural and Health services, Master Foody Moody's food-buying cooperatives, Vision of Mulund Institute educational services for young people, cooperative business associations, and the death and dying ministry.

The Religious Necessity of Cooperative Human Community

from
The Truly Human New World-Culture Of Unbroken Real-God-Man
by Avatar Adi Da Samraj

Here Avatar Adi Da discusses the essential role of cooperative sacred association in religious life:

There is no such thing as right and true religion without cooperative human culture. Cooperative sacred culture is the necessary theatre wherein right and true religious responsibilities and activities can take place.

Over time, the common understanding of religion and of religious responsibilities has become abstracted and dogmatized (and made merely exoteric), such that religion has been made to seem to be a merely personal (or merely subjective, and private) endeavor. Thus, in this "late-time" (or "dark" epoch), conventional (and merely exoteric) religion has become deficient as a true culture.

The abstract State, or the broad social apparatus of politics and economics, is an inherently secular domain. When the people become tied exclusively to the secular environment of the State, they become fragmented into a mass of mere individuals, controlled by great (and, inherently, indifferent) political and economic forces. Therefore, right and true (and, necessarily, esoteric) religion must function not only in terms of the Teaching of Ultimate Spiritual Realization of the Self-Evidently Divine Reality and Truth, but right and true (and not merely exoteric) religion must also function as the practical foundation of right (intimate and collective) human relationships. Therefore, the Teachings of right and true (and, necessarily, esoteric) religion must become the basic (or sacred) foundation of the totality of human life. That is to say, right and true religion must (necessarily) become the sacred cultural instrument whereby human individuals collectively create cooperative human order—both in terms of intimate (or local) community and in terms of a global union of all human communities.

In this "late-time" (or "dark" epoch), conventional religion tends to create (and to function as) an institutional order, but it (generally) fails to create a practical cooperative order (or true cooperative culture). The institutions of conventional religion tend to organize the attention and the resources of people in much the same manner as the modern-day secular State. That is to say, merely "institutional" (and exoteric) religion fragments the inherent unity (and, thus, the necessary cooperative culture) of humankind into a chaotic mass of merely competing individuals. Therefore, conventional (and merely exoteric) religion fails to be right and true religion—not only because it fails to Reveal Reality and Truth (or Real God), but because it also fails to oblige people to create real, right, and true religious culture (involving mutual cooperation, mutual responsibility, and mutual dependence).

Practitioners of right and true religion must (and, necessarily, do) orient themselves to the free creation of a sacred cooperative culture. Truly, the inherent obligations of right and true religion can be fulfilled only by those who are sufficiently religiously mature to be responsible in the practical theatre of human relationships. Therefore, practitioners of true religion should (optimally) live in daily cooperative circumstances, wherein there are constant opportunities to be tested and to be creative in relationships with other like practitioners.

It is only among the right and true practitioners of right and true (and, necessarily, esoteric) religion that the fullest right human agreements are possible—agreements which oblige each and all to accept the many daily practical conditions of a fully cooperative and completely sacred human culture of devotees of Reality and Truth (Which Is the only Real God).

Study of Avatar Adi Da's Divine Teaching

All devotees of Avatar Adi Da are called to the discipline of daily study of His Divine Wisdom-Teaching. His Heart-Word, Revealed in twenty-three Divine "Source-Texts", is an unprecedented manifestation. It is the literal Communication—direct and untouched—of the Incarnate Divine Person.

Everything about Adidam that is described in this introductory book is fully and elaborately Communicated by Avatar Adi Da Himself in His own Word. To bring oneself to Avatar Adi Da's Wisdom-Teaching in a surrendered, receptive disposition, is to be engaged with Him in what He Calls a "Living Conversation"—one that addresses you directly in your present moment of awareness and devotional practice and also Calls you to grow further in ego-transcending response to Him.

In His Divine Word, Avatar Adi Da Confesses the Nature of His own Divine Being and Instructs human beings in the process of Realizing His Divine Condition. His primary "Source-Text", *The Dawn Horse Testament,* is a uniquely detailed and complete description of the unfolding process of Divine Liberation, lived through the devotional and Spiritual relationship to Him. In *The Dawn Horse Testament*, He describes what that process requires at every developmental stage, up to and including Divine Enlightenment—which is Spiritual surrender to Him to the degree of most perfectly Realizing Him, beyond any trace of separateness.

Avatar Adi Da's Divine Heart-Word has emerged out of the Ordeal of His entire Life. Everything of which He speaks has been thoroughly tested and proven in His own body-mind. To study the Divine "Source-Texts" of Avatar Adi Da is profoundly inspiring, and also confronting to the ego. One must persist, stay with Him, feel deeper. To truly receive His Message in His Divine Books, one must bring one's full feeling-attention to Him, and allow Him to purify you of ego-mind. In that process, He Reveals Himself to you.

AVATAR ADI DA SAMRAJ: My Word is Sealed—It is Complete. My twenty-three "Source-Texts" are Made, and Done. Every word and comma and quotation mark was made and approved and made perfect by Me. What was Made is Good, and Complete, and Whole, and Fine, and Great.

I have Done what I had to Do.

So take the arms of My twenty-three "Source-Texts", and the life of this Way of Adidam in My Avataric Divine Company, and live it rightly, truly, fully, fully devotionally, and bring it as My Gift to all of humankind. And be the seed whereby this Transformation can occur.

—December 15, 1997

The disciplines Given by Avatar Adi Da enable you to conform every moment and aspect of life to the ever-deepening process of devotional Communion with Him, progressively transcending all limits on the Realization of His "Bright" Divine Condition. This is the Second Fundamental of the True World-Religion of Adidam. ■

True Spiritual Life Requires Profound Purification of Your Ordinary Human Existence

from
The Dawn Horse Testament Of The Ruchira Avatar

In this excerpt from chapter 28 of The Dawn Horse Testament Of The Ruchira Avatar, *Avatar Adi Da describes how the re-patterning of the activities of the body-mind is necessary for and supports growth in the Spiritual process of Adidam.*

As My Devotee, It Is Essential That You Deal Appropriately With The Foundation Matters Of ordinary human life, Such That the body-mind Is (Thus and Thereby) Fundamentally Purified. By Establishing the body-mind In The By-Me-Given Basic functional, practical, relational, and Cultural Disciplines, You Are Moved Beyond Preoccupation With (and Confinement To) the gross ego (and The Total Pattern Of social egoity), and Re-Oriented To The (By-Me-and-As-Me-Avatarically-Self-Revealed) Divine Self-Condition. In Order To Truly Grow In My Avataric Divine Company, There Must Be A Turning Of The Faculties—From The Obsession With "money, food, and sex" and social egoity, To Me. . . .

True Spiritual Life Requires Profound Purification Of Your ordinary human existence, and (Thus) Profound Purification Of The Principal Faculties (Of body, emotion, mind, and breath). That Purification Is, In Part, Accomplished Through Your Consistent Application Of The By-Me-Given Basic functional, practical, relational, and Cultural Disciplines. At The Most Profound Level, That Purification

Is Accomplished Only By My Spiritual Invasion Of My To-Me-Surrendered Devotee—and That Great and Most Profound Process Of Purification Continues Even Into and Throughout The Only-By-Me Revealed and Given Seventh Stage Of Life.

There Are Specific Gifts Of Practice That You, As My Devotee, Must Bring To Me—From The Beginning Of Your Embrace Of The . . . Way Of Adidam. You Must Bring To Me The Gift Of Your Devotional Resort To Me, Based On Your Heart-Recognition Of Me. And You Must Bring To Me The Gift Of Your Fulfillment Of The By-Me-Given Basic functional, practical, relational, and Cultural Disciplines—Which Disciplines Establish The Necessary Foundation Of Purification and Equanimity, and (In Due Course) The Preparedness To Be Initiated, By Me, Into The Real Spiritual Process Of Devotional Relationship To Me, and Which Disciplines (Altogether) Re-Orient The Totality Of the body-mind To The Great Purpose Of Realizing Me.

Merely To Be a functional social ego Has Nothing To Do With Real Spiritual Life. There Must Be A Turning-Over Of the life From The "money, food, and sex" Preoccupations With Which people ordinarily busy themselves. As My Devotee, You Must Involve All Of The psycho-physical Faculties In The Sadhana Of Turning To Me. Do Not Imagine That It Is Sufficient Merely To "Re-Model" (or Idealize and Systematize) Your Preoccupation With gross egoic (or social egoic) life On The Basis Of A Series Of Prescriptive Disciplines. Only The Fundamental ego-Surrendering Practice Of Devotionally Turning To Me (or Ruchira Avatara Bhakti Yoga) Is Sufficient. The Disciplining Of Your functional, practical, and relational life Is A Matter Of Conforming (or Fitting) the body-mind (in its functional, practical, and relational sphere) To The Turning Of The Faculties To Me. . . .

As My Devotee, You Must Transform Your "money,

food, and sex" life and Your social life. It Is Not Necessary To "Leave the world" (In Some Absolute Sense) In Order For This Transformation To Occur, but It Is Essential That You Consistently Participate In The Sacred Domain Of The Culture Of Adidam. Through Such Participation, You Must (In every day) "Retrieve" time From its Usual Patterning With The Preoccupations Of "money, food, and sex" and social egoity. And You Must (Thereby) Simplify Everything functional, practical, and relational—Everything To Do With "money, food, and sex" and social egoity—and "Retrieve" time From all of that, For The Sacred (or Set-Apart) Exercise Of Turning The Faculties To Me.

In The Only-By-Me Revealed and Given Way Of Adidam, It Is Not the body-mind but egoity itself That Must Be Renounced—By Means Of Right Devotion To Me, Practiced moment to moment. And All The Renunciation That Comes About (In the body-mind itself) Occurs By My Avataric Divine Spiritual Grace. As My Devotee, You Must Embrace The Fundamental Disciplines I Have Given To You—but The Profundities Of Renunciation Come About By My Avataric Divine Spiritual Grace. Renunciation Of the ego-"I" Is A Divine Spiritual Gift From Me—Just As Realization Of Me (Myself) Is A Divine Spiritual Gift From Me.

Your Patterns Of Dis-Ease and self-Indulgence Do Obstruct The Spiritual Process In My Avataric Divine Company—but Those Patterns Will Be Purified, If You Persist In Truly Turning To Me and Rightly Disciplining the body-mind. You Will Voluntarily Relinquish Them In The Fullness Of Spiritually Receiving Me. At Some Point, It Will Hurt Too Much To Continue Enacting (and Indulging In) Those Patterns. Then, It Will Be Self-Evident That A Particular Pattern or Tendency or Habit Has Run Its Course, Ceasing To Be "interesting"—and It Will Fall Away In Your Free Relinquishment Of It.

Ultimately, everything conditional Must Be Relinquished. In Due Course, death Is Inevitable. Therefore, All Of Your (Total psycho-physical) ego-Patterning—gross, subtle, and causal—Must, Ultimately, Be Transcended. However, This Total Relinquishment Is Not Required To Occur In a single instant. This Relinquishment Occurs In A Right (Progressive) Order, In The Course Of The Real Spiritual Process In My Avataric Divine Company. The More You Are Spiritually In-Filled By Me, The More Of Your ego-Patterning Is Purified and (Thereby) Relinquished (or Renounced).

This By-My-Avataric-Divine-Spiritual-Grace-Given Renunciation Occurs From head To toe. The Purification Is Accomplished By Means Of My Avataric Divine Spiritual Invasion. Therefore, Renunciation In The Way Of Adidam Is Not an idealistic (and self-Involved) "program", Requiring You To "Do" Something "To" the body-mind. The Fundamental Disciplines Of The Way Of Adidam Are Simply A Matter Of Right Life—Simply The Means Whereby the body-mind Is Established In The Yogic Equanimity Of Devotionally Turning To Me. When You Are (As A Total psycho-physical Whole) Fully Thus Established, My Avataric Divine Spiritual Invasion Occurs—Bringing About The Purification and Transformation Of the (Total psycho-physical) body-mind. Through Your Constant Devotional Turning To Me, I Am Moved To Give You My Divine Spiritual Gifts. Receiving My Avataric Divine Spiritual Blessing-Transmission Is Not An Automatic "Given". My Avataric Divine Spiritual Blessing-Transmission Is A Gift That Is Volunteered By Me In Response To Your Right and True Devotion To Me.

To Clearly Receive Me Spiritually Is Utterly life-Transforming. To Actually Experience Me Spiritually—Coming Upon You From <u>Outside</u> and <u>Beyond</u> Yourself—Is A Miraculous (and, Ultimately, Incomprehensible) Event. And The Real Spiritual Reception (and Spiritual Experience) Of Me Is The <u>Only</u> Absolute Proof Of The Divine. Everything

Else (That Might Be Adduced As Evidence Of The Divine) Is mere "talk".

When You Experience Me Spiritually, You Are Necessarily Transformed. To Experience Me Spiritually Is A Divine Discovery That Effectively Converts the being. When You (Thus) Discover Me, You Become Capable Of "Locating" Me Spiritually. Then I Can Do My (Purifying and Awakening) Spiritual Work With You—and The Signs Of That Work Will Spontaneously Manifest In Your body-mind, More and More Over time.

What You Have On Your mind Is Boring and Unsatisfactory. Your thoughts and Your self-Manipulations Are Fruitless and Dis-Heartening—Regardless Of their content.

To Be Fallen Upon By My Self-Evident Divine "Brightness" Is The Only Satisfaction. It Is The Only Cure For Doubt and For All The Fear and Sorrow and Anger Of This Heart-Murdering Event here.

Without My Avataric Divine Spiritual Invasion, This Is Unrelieved Suffering. In and Of Itself, This Is A Horror, a Terrible place of endings.

You Cannot think Your Way Out Of it. At the moment of Your death, There Is No mere thought You Can Have In mind That Will Give You Peace.

Only My Sheer and Absolute Avataric Divine Spiritual Presence Solves The Heart Of My Devotee.

THIRD FUNDAMENTAL

The "Conscious Process" of Attention and the "Conductivity" of Energy

Supporting the Primary Practice

The fundamental practice in Adidam is always the practice of devotion to Avatar Adi Da, or Ruchira Avatara Bhakti Yoga. As we saw in the First Fundamental, this practice of devotion to Avatar Adi Da is exercised by allowing the four faculties (of mind, emotion, body, and breath) to be effortlessly turned to Him by means of His Spiritual Attractiveness.

When you are feeling Avatar Adi Da's Spiritual Attractiveness, you are naturally moved to respond to Him. You are naturally moved to do whatever allows Communion with Him to remain constant and to become even deeper.

Avatar Adi Da has given two basic forms of technical practice—that deepen that always first and fundamental practice of Ruchira Avatara Bhakti Yoga. These practices are the "conscious process" and "conductivity". The "conscious process" relates to (and supports) the turning of the faculty of attention to Avatar Adi Da. And "conductivity" practice relates to (and supports) the turning of the energy-related faculties (of body, emotion, and breath) to Him.

The unique technical practices of the "conscious process" and "conductivity" are complementary and mutually supportive—and of equal importance relative to the total practice of Adidam. But they are only to be engaged responsively—that is, on the basis of mind, emotion, body, and breath being <u>already</u> turned to Avatar

Adi Da. In other words, they are ways of supporting and magnifying the freely received Gift of devotion, not ways of "getting" devotion to "happen". This crucial distinction is what makes the practices of the "conscious process" and "conductivity" a matter of the relationship to Avatar Adi Da—rather than a matter of techniques, engaged independent of the relationship to Him.

The "Conscious Process": Simple Name-Invocation and the Two Devotional Ways

A principal form of the turning of attention to Avatar Adi Da, engaged by all His devotees, is the simple Invocation of Him by Name. This can be done either silently (reciting His Name simply in the mind) or aloud. Such Invocation can also be done using a mala (or rosary) or in occasions of devotional chanting or worshipful expression. In this way, you constantly re-invoke the direct relationship with Him in His bodily Form.

Over the years of His Teaching-Work, Avatar Adi Da found that people's devotional response to Him was exhibited in two basic modes. So He developed two distinct forms of the "conscious process", in order to optimally serve these two types of people. Neither of these two forms of the "conscious process" is superior to the other. It is simply a matter of each individual devotee determining which form is most effective in his or her case.

The first form of the "conscious process" is called "the Devotional Way of Insight", which is taken up by those who find that the exercise of insight into their own activity of self-contraction (combined with the fundamental practice of turning to Avatar Adi Da), is (for them) the most effective means of Communing with Avatar Adi Da.

The second form of the "conscious process" is called "the Devotional Way of Faith", which is taken up by those who find that the exercise of faith in Avatar Adi Da (combined with the fundamental practice of turning to Him) is (for them) the most effective means of Communing with Avatar Adi Da.

Of course, all practitioners of Adidam must exercise both insight (into the self-contraction) and faith (in Avatar Adi Da). But each person will find that one or the other—either insight or faith—is a particularly effective means for magnifying Communion with Avatar Adi Da. As a beginning practitioner of Adidam, you go through an initial period of "testing and proving" in order to determine whether the Devotional Way of Faith or the Devotional Way of Insight is the optimum manner of practice for you.

The Devotional Way of Insight

The form of the "conscious process" practiced in the Devotional Way of Insight is known as "self-Enquiry"—in other words, enquiring of oneself relative to one's own activity of self-contraction. This form of the "conscious process" involves silently "remembering" a single, very simple question: "Avoiding relationship?" This particular exercise—which condenses Avatar Adi Da's entire "consideration" relative to the self-contraction into two simple words—was spontaneously developed by Him during the years of His Sadhana (previous to His Divine Re-Awakening).

The devotee who is practicing (or experimenting with) the Devotional Way of Insight enquires, at random in daily life, and during periods of meditation: "Avoiding relationship?" You do this as you notice anything—beings, things, ideas, or feelings—arising in your body or mind. The purpose of the exercise is not to "answer" the question, but simply to observe, understand, and feel beyond the activity of self-contraction. In this manner, one ceases to "avoid relationship" and is released into present-time relatedness and devotional Communion with Avatar Adi Da. This is the "conscious process" by which the practitioner of the Devotional Way of Insight deepens Communion with Avatar Adi Da.

The Devotional Way of Faith

Although all practitioners in the Way of Adidam have a faith-response to Avatar Adi Da, the Devotional Way of Faith is taken up by those whose faith in Him directly "carries" them beyond the self-contraction, without requiring the specific intensive exercise of insight.

The form of the "conscious process" practiced in the Devotional Way of Faith is the heart-felt Invocation of Avatar Adi Da via specific forms of His Name. In the earlier stages of the Devotional Way of Faith, such Invocation is done by the (generally silent) repetition of a Mantra. (Avatar Adi Da has Given eighty different Mantras, all of which are derived from His Names and Titles. Each beginning practitioner of the Devotional Way of Faith chooses one of the eighty mantras to use in daily practice of the "conscious process".) This practice of invocation via a Mantra is known as "Ruchira Avatara Naama Japa"—or the repeated invocation ("Japa") of the Name ("Naama") of the Ruchira Avatar. And that practice can be associated with "counting" the beads of a rosary (or mala).

When the practitioner of the Devotional Way of Faith reaches the point of full technical responsibility for the consistent reception of Avatar Adi Da's Spiritual Transmission, the form of the "conscious process" then becomes the "Prayer of Remembrance", which is invocation of Avatar Adi Da simply via His Name "Da", associated with a technically detailed practice of breathing-reception of Him.

The Ultimate Form of the "Conscious Process"

When a practitioner has come to the point of practicing in the most mature stages of Adidam (the stages which Avatar Adi Da calls the "Perfect Practice"), the form of the "conscious process" changes for everyone. Whether you were previously practicing the Devotional Way of Insight or the Devotional Way of Faith, you now take up the profound and technically detailed practice of "Feeling-Enquiry". "Feeling-Enquiry" is the "conscious process" that allows the practitioner to be "carried", by Avatar Adi Da's Divine Spiritual Grace, entirely beyond ego—into Divine Enlightenment, or most perfect Realization of Avatar Adi Da's "Bright" Divine Self-Condition.

In His twenty-three "Source-Texts", Avatar Adi Da Gives detailed Instruction on all forms of the "conscious process" engaged in the Way of Adidam.

"Conductivity" Practice

"Conductivity" practice relates to the domain of energy, rather than the domain of consciousness and attention. Specifically, "conductivity" practice first relates to the domain of natural life-energy, then, after the devotee is Spiritually Initiated by Avatar Adi Da, to the domain of Spirit-Energy as well. (Natural life-energy, or "etheric" energy, is the life-force that can be felt surrounding and infusing the human physical body. The emotional dimension of the being is a manifestation of this natural life-energy. Spirit-Energy is the All-Pervading Energy of the Divine. Avatar Adi Da's Spiritual Transmission is the Transmission of the Divine Spirit-Energy.*)

In broad terms, "conductivity" practice includes the full range of life-positive disciplines relative to right diet, sexuality, "conscious exercise", service, and cooperative culture—for all of these basic disciplines serve your body's ability to conduct natural life-energy and (in due course) Avatar Adi Da's Divine Spirit-Energy.

In addition to these basic disciplines, Avatar Adi Da has Given specific technical "conductivity" exercises that allow you to responsibly control and direct the flow of natural life-energy and (in due course) His Divine Spirit-Energy in your body. These technical exercises are the indispensable complement to your practice of the "conscious process". (The "conductivity" practices are the same for all devotees, whether they practice the Devotional Way of Insight or the Devotional Way of Faith.)

The technical form of "conductivity" initially practiced in the Way of Adidam has three parts:

- heart-surrender to Avatar Adi Da, while practicing feeling-radiation in all directions from the heart
- relaxing the frontal line of the body, from the crown of the head to the bodily base (at the perineum)
- breathing in a process of inhalation-reception and exhalation-release

*For a more complete discussion of Avatar Adi Da's Spirit-Energy, see the discussion of searchless Beholding of Avatar Adi Da and His "Ruchira Shaktipat" in the Fourth Fundamental.

This simple three-part exercise acts as a powerful means for the body to open, relax, and (thereby) freely circulate and conduct energy. You establish this basic practice of three-part "conductivity" as a beginning devotee. Thereafter, your responsibility for "conductivity" grows to include the "conducting" of Spirit-Energy, once you have been Initiated by Avatar Adi Da into the Spiritual dimension of practice.

In His twenty-three "Source-Texts", Avatar Adi Da Gives detailed Instruction on how to practice "conductivity" of both the natural life-energy and His Divine Spirit-Energy. And, when the practitioner reaches the most mature stages of Adidam, he or she is initiated into the "radical" form of Spirit-"conductivity", which Avatar Adi Da has reserved for His Spiritually most qualified devotees (and which is only communicated privately, never through published texts).

Meditation and the Process of Awakening

The "conscious process" and "conductivity" practice are engaged most intensively during formal periods of meditation. Meditation in the Way of Adidam is a concentrated occasion of turning the faculties of the body-mind to Avatar Adi Da, with no other distractions. True meditation in the Way of Adidam is a Gift from Avatar Adi Da, of in-depth Communion with Him, rather than any kind of self-motivated technique.

Formal meditative practice in the Way of Adidam takes place in sacred settings—set-apart Communion Halls that, through devotees' persistent Invocation of Avatar Adi Da, become imbued with the feeling-sense of His Spiritual Presence. The basic meditative discipline in Adidam is two formal periods of meditation daily. You start by adapting to two periods of 30 minutes each, and then you adapt to longer periods—60-90 minutes in the morning (upon arising), and 60 minutes during the early evening or just before retiring to sleep.

As your practice matures in the Way of Adidam, meditation becomes an ever-deepening occasion of Communion with Avatar Adi Da, and it becomes your primary daily "food". It is the key practice in the process of "waking up" to the Divine Reality:

Simple (Natural) arousal From the dreaming state To the waking state of the body-mind Immediately (If Only Naturally, or conditionally) awakens You From Identification With the Problems and Illusions You Seemed To Suffer or Seek In the dreaming state. Just So, In The Only-By-Me Revealed and Given Way Of Adidam, Meditation (and, Especially, Deep Meditation) Directly (and More and More Profoundly, and Then Inherently, and Inherently Most Perfectly, or Un-conditionally) Awakens You From Identification With the Problems and Illusions You Seem (or Seemed) To Suffer or Seek In the waking state. Likewise, In The Way Of Adidam, Meditation (and, Especially, Deep Meditation) Directly (and More and More Profoundly—and Then Inherently, and Inherently Most Perfectly, or Un-conditionally) Awakens You From Identification With (and all limitation by) the waking state itself, the dreaming state itself, and the sleeping state itself. Indeed, The Great Process Of Meditation In The Way Of Adidam (Beginning With Simple Feeling-Contemplation Of My Avatarically-Born Bodily Human Divine Form, My Avatarically Self-Transmitted Spiritual, and Always Blessing, Divine Presence, and My Avatarically Self-Revealed, and Very, and Transcendental, and Perfectly Subjective, and Inherently Spiritual, and Inherently egoless, and Inherently Perfect, and Self-Evidently Divine State—and Progressing, On That Basis, Via All The Necessary and Appropriate Practices and Developmental Processes In The Way Of Adidam) Is A Total and (Most Ultimately) Inherent (and Inherently Most Perfect) Awakening From the Problems, Illusions, sufferings, Searches, limitations, experiences, knowledge, and conditional self-Identity Associated With all Possible states Of conditional (or psycho-physical) Existence.

In The Only-By-Me Revealed and Given Way Of Adidam, Meditation . . . Is (In Right Conjunction With The Full Range Of All The Only-By-Me Revealed and Given functional, practical, relational, and Cultural Disciplines) The Principal (Progressively

Effective) Means Whereby conceptual philosophy (or "God"-Talk) and limited insight Become (or Are Directly Transcended In) Spiritual, Transcendental, and (Most Ultimately) Divine Self-Realization. . . .

In The Only-By-Me Revealed and Given Way Of Adidam, Meditation Is Not A Technique, but A Gift (From Me)—and Even All The Technical Forms (or By-Me-Given Technical Exercises) Of Meditation Practice In The Way Of Adidam Are, Truly, Only Secondary Means, To Be Applied For The Sake Of Serving The Fundamental Practice (Of Devotional Resort To Me, and Devotional Contemplation Of Me, and Devotional Response To Me, and Devotional and Meditative Cooperation With Me).

The Way Of Adidam (and Meditation In The Way Of Adidam) Is A Relationship—Not Merely A System Of Techniques.

—Avatar Adi Da Samraj
The Dawn Horse Testament Of The Ruchira Avatar

Sacramental Worship

In Adidam, sacramental worship is ecstatic, actively expressed Communion with Avatar Adi Da—including worship of His bodily Form (usually via a photographic representation), devotional chanting, prayer, and recitation of His Avataric Divine Word.

Sacramental worship is known as "puja". The principal form of puja (the "Ṛuchira Avatara Puja") is done every day, following morning meditation. The practice of puja in Adidam is a unique development of traditional practices of Guru-devotion. In this form of worship, the devotee installs Avatar Adi Da before the heart, via a specific ceremony of washing and anointing a photographic representation of His physical Form (called a "Murti") and/or a pair of His Empowered sandals (called "Padukas").

In The Only-By-Me Revealed and Given Way Of Adidam, A Sacramental Act (Of Any Kind) Is A Special Sacred Performance. That Act Is The "Opposite" (or, Really, The Complement) Of Meditation—In The Sense That, While Meditation Involves

Intentional Transcending Of bodily Consciousness In Devotional Communion With Me, The Sacramental Act Intentionally Includes bodily Consciousness In A Kind Of Rapturous, Artful Enactment Of Devotional Communion With Me (Wherein You Must Constantly Maintain attention In The Context Of the body and its relations—but In The Manner Of A Sacred Performance, and Not In casual, conventional Terms). Because In Sacramental Activities You Are (Variously) Always Intentionally and Outwardly Active (bodily, vocally, and so forth), You Never (Except In The Event Of A Spontaneous Swoon) Abandon bodily Consciousness. Nevertheless, In The Way Of Adidam, You Must Allow Your body-mind To Be Completely Absorbed In ego-Surrendering, ego-Forgetting, and (More and More) ego-Transcending Communion With Me Through All Your Sacramental (or Right bodily) Activities. In The Way Of Adidam, Every Event and Kind Of Sacramental (or Right bodily) Activity Is To Be An Event (or A Form) Of That Aspect Of Your Total Practice Of The Way Of Adidam That Functions To Balance (or Complement) The Effect Of Meditation—and (Altogether) The Constant Discipline Of Converting all bodily (or Outward) activity Into True Sacramental Activity Must Constantly Oblige You To Rightly (and Sacredly, or Truly Religiously, or Culturally) Orient all the functional, practical, and relational performances of daily life (which You, Otherwise, Tend Not To Turn Into A Sacramental, or Sacred, or Religious, or Cultural Performance, but which Are, In Fact, Supposed To Be Such).

—Avatar Adi Da Samraj
The Dawn Horse Testament Of The Ruchira Avatar

The practices of puja and meditation in the Way of Adidam are essential expressions of Satsang—life in the Heart-Company of Avatar Adi Da. Through the process of Satsang, Avatar Adi Da Awakens you from the dream of ordinary life.

The fundamental practice of devotion to Avatar Adi Da is supported and magnified by the unique technical practices of the "conscious process" and "conductivity". This is the Third Fundamental of the True World-Religion of Adidam. ■

Awakening from the Dream of Ordinary Life

from "The Gorilla Sermon"
by Avatar Adi Da Samraj

This Talk comes from the early 1970s, during the first year of Avatar Adi Da's Teaching-Work. It is included in the collection of classic Talks from that period, The Divine Siddha-Method Of The Ruchira Avatar. *In these Talks, Avatar Adi Da particularly focused on the fundamentals of Spiritual practice in His Company: the devotional relationship to Him, and the understanding of one's activity of self-contraction.*

AVATAR ADI DA SAMRAJ: It is really a simple matter. The usual person thinks: "This body and its psyche are dying. This world is dying. Everyone is suffering, everyone is seeking. There is mortality, there is frustration and limitation." But none of that is Truth. Those interpretations are not Truth. The world itself is not Truth—nor is life, nor psyche and body, nor death, nor experience. No event is (itself) Truth. All that arises is an appearance to Consciousness Itself, a modification of the Conscious Light That Is Always Already the Case. All of this is a dream, if you like. It is an appearance in Consciousness Itself. Truth is Very Consciousness (or the One and Only Conscious Light) Itself. Truth is to all of this what the waking state is to the dreaming state. If you awaken, you do not have to do anything about the condition you may have suffered or enjoyed in the dream state. What happened within the dream is suddenly not your present condition. It is of no consequence any longer, once you are awake. If you persist in dreaming, and your point of view remains that of the dreamer and the dreamer's role within the dream, then your possible actions are numberless. But none of them will "work". They will simply occupy you in the dream. They will modify the dream state, but no action in the dream is the equivalent of waking. There are simply forms of fascination, of occupation, of seeking—until you awaken. Truth is simply Waking, No-illusion. Truth is not a condition within this appearance. Truth has nothing whatsoever to do with the mind, regardless of whether the mind is expanded or contracted.

Perception is simply what it obviously is. There is no reason for any perception to change in order for Truth to Appear as a consequence. The dream does not have to be changed in any manner for the waking person to feel that he or she is awake. There is not anything that has to happen to the dream. Only waking is necessary. To one who is awake, the dream is obvious. There is no illusion, no suffering, no implication—regardless of what appeared in the dream. A blue god, a dirty old drunk, the gorilla of death—it makes no difference. It makes a difference within the circumstances of the dream, to those who are dreaming. But to the one who is awake, it no longer makes any difference. Perception, waking consciousness, is obvious if you are truly Awake. If you are asleep—if you do not understand, if understanding evades you—there is nothing obvious about this at all. Then life is a very serious predicament—very serious. What do you have in such a case? "A few more years and everything is dead." It does not make any difference what the drama is, or how you manage to amuse yourself during that time.

There is One Who is Wide Awake while He Appears in the dream of ordinary waking life. By His Mere Presence, simply by not supporting the dream, He Awakens others. He is the True Guru, Who I Am. The significance of My Avataric Divine Work is not in anything I do within the dream. I simply do not support it. I do not live as it. I do not believe it. I do not take it seriously. Apparently, I can feel and act as I please. I persist in the common or ordinary manner. But I do not support the dream. I do not live from its point of view. I do not live its structure to others. I do not live this contraction to others, this avoidance of relationship, this separate-self-sense. Simply because I live in this manner, others tend to become Awake. But while they are Awakening, they persist in dreaming to various degrees. Forms of the dream persist. The search persists. Often, they get a little distance from it, it seems to break up at times, seems to disappear. It becomes vague, it becomes uninteresting, it becomes un-serious, it becomes serious again. They play.

You are just beginning to wake up. Satsang with Me is the dream wherein I Appear. Now it is as if you are beginning to wake up in your room. You are in bed, and it is morning. There are a few things you begin to notice which indicate that you are in another state. Those who are Waking in Truth begin to notice something. They begin to recognize the signs. They begin to recognize the activity of dreaming. They begin to sense something very unusual about Me. Before their actual Awakening, I appear as all kinds of things to them. I suggest all kinds of fantastic things. All the things they can imagine while they dream—everything unbelievable—is what they think I am. I may appear to be extraordinary, a doer of famous things. I may appear playfully as that. But I am simply Awake. There is not anything that is happening. There is not anything that has been accomplished. All I have been is Awake.

I am like the sunlight in the morning. I intensify the light of morning until you awaken. Until the light awakens you, even the Light of Consciousness Itself, you continue to dream, try to survive within the dream, manipulate yourself within the dream, pursue all kinds of goals, searches—none of which Awakens you. All ordinary means only console you and distract you within the dream.

I Myself, the One Who would Awaken you, am not an individual within the dream. I Am your Very Self-Condition. I Am the Real, the Conscious Light, the True Waking State, the True Divine Heart—Breaking Through the force of dreaming. It is not that you are some poor person who needs some other poor person to help you out. It may appear to be so within the dream—but, essentially, I Am your own Most Prior Self-Nature Appearing within the dream in order to Awaken you. I Am your Awakening, and your Always Already Conscious State.

Even while dreaming, you may experience suggestions of waking. You may become momentarily aware of the body, momentarily aware of lying in bed. For a moment, the images of the dream may stop. Just so, I Myself (within the world) Am truly your Real Consciousness. My Avatarically-Born Person in the world is like an image in a dream. But, in fact, I am more like your own moments of wakening awareness that move you into the waking state. I am not some separateness, some individual. I Am Consciousness Itself, Reality Itself.

No images. Images, blackness, brilliance—all these things are appearances to Consciousness. They are objects. There is not anything that needs to happen to them for Consciousness Itself to exist. There is not anything that needs to happen within the dream in order to verify Waking. Waking is its own Fullness. Once one is Awake, anything can appear. True Awakeness is the foundation, the support, the Very Nature of this world-appearance. Consciousness Itself is not antagonistic to this world or to any form within it. Consciousness Itself is the Truth of all appearance, disappearance, or non-appearance. Even when Consciousness Itself is Realized, human life continues. Perhaps human life is enjoyed even more. It is rightly and effectively used. It becomes functional to an extraordinary degree.

The usual person barely functions at all—a couple of good days a month. The rest of the time, he or she is either trying to be healed or else indulging in self-exploitation and then trying to "get straight", to "get with it". Every now and then there is a little clarity, when the person just stands up, walks across the room, opens the door, and goes outside. The rest of the month is spent dreaming and thinking—when just to walk across the room is part of an enormous search, an unkind adventure, a struggle for victory against great odds. But all the person is doing is simple things, simple functions.

One who understands, who is Awake, functions very well under whatever conditions appear. Those conditions may be forms of this waking world, or they may be subtle forms, subtle worlds—any of the possible forms. Under all conditions, understanding is appropriate. There is no experience, no state, that is (itself) identical to Truth. Just so, the Truth is not different from any form of experience, any state of conscious awareness. Truth is the Truth of all of that.

I am a kind of irritation to My devotees. You cannot sleep with a dog barking in your ear—at least, most people cannot! There is some sort of noise to which everyone is sensitive, and it will keep them awake. I Am a constant Wakening Sound. I am always annoying people with this demand to stay Awake, to Wake Up. I do not seduce you within the dream. I do not exploit your seeking. I am always offending your search and your preference for unconsciousness. I show no interest in all of that. I Criticize it mightily. I am always Doing Something Prior to the mind. I always Act to Return you from the mind, from fascination.

I am not what the dreamer thinks I am. The dreamer thinks I must have a certain appearance, say and do certain things, have certain magical powers, produce certain magical effects. The dreamer associates all kinds of glorious and magical things with Me. But I am always performing the Awakening act, putting an end to the dream. Therefore, I do not satisfy the seeker. Those that come to be satisfied are offended. They are not satisfied. They feel empty, they do not feel their questions have been answered, they do not feel they have been shown the Way. They came for some "thing".

Within the dream, the dreamer is always being satisfied by the Guru. The dreamer climbs up on the top of the mountain, and the Guru is sitting in a cave. The Guru hands the dreamer a little silver box. When the dreamer opens the box, there is a blue diamond in it. The dreamer takes it out and swallows it. Then the dreamer's body explodes into a million suns, and the dreamer shoots off into the universe! But, in Reality, the True Guru does not function in that manner. The True Guru is not noticed by someone who is seeking for such satisfaction, who is looking for the "signs" of the Guru, who is "hunting" the Guru. The True Guru does not assume any particular visibility that can be counted on. The True Guru is likely to remain unnoticed. People tend not to notice or value someone who is simply Awake. They are looking for the one who has the blue and yellow light over his or her head. All of this—until they become dissatisfied with the search. When they start being sensitive to the suffering of their own search, they begin to feel simply desperate. Then all that is left is this contraction I have so often described. When the search begins to wind down, and you begin to realize you are suffering, then you become sensitive to Me. You become attentive to the Very Nature of the One Who is Awake.

It is stated in the traditional writings that, of all the things you can do to Realize Freedom, the best thing you can do, the greatest thing you can do, is to spend time in the Company of one who is Awake. For My devotee, that is Satsang with Me—living in relationship to Me and in the company of My devotees. All other activities are secondary. And Satsang with Me is not a strategic method, not an exercise or meditative technique you apply to yourself. It is simply the natural and appropriate Condition. It is Reality Itself. Satsang with Me is (Itself) Truth, or Enlightenment. There are no other means given to My devotees.

There is not anything that you can do to save yourself, to become Enlightened, to become Realized. Nothing whatsoever. If there were something, I would tell you—but there is not anything. This is because people always approach the Truth from the point of view of the search. Human beings seek the Truth. But the search is (itself) a reaction to the dilemma, an expression of this presumed separation, this avoidance of relationship. So none of this seeking—not anything you can "do"—becomes or attains the Truth.

All the means of transformation belong to the Truth Itself, to the Divine Person, to the True Divine Heart. Therefore, Satsang with Me is (Itself) the only sadhana, the only true Spiritual practice. Living, working, sitting with Me is sadhana. It is meditation. It is Realization.

To Enjoy Truth is simply to be Awake. I have often used the contrast between the waking state and the dreaming state to symbolize the difference between "radical" understanding and all the forms of seeking. All attainments, all forms of cognition, all forms of mind, however sublime, belong within the dream. When extraordinary (and even miraculous) conditions are actually enjoyed or experienced, they reveal themselves to be essentially of the same nature as the ordinary experience of suffering that provoked the search to begin with. In My Own Case, there is no consolation in samadhis, or trance states, no consolation in visions, no consolation in going to other worlds, no consolation in any Realization that can be attained. At last, when understanding is most perfect, it becomes obvious that all that has ever occurred has been a modification of Consciousness Itself (or the One and Only Divine Conscious Light). This entire thing that has been upsetting you—all this movement, all this seeking, all this attainment, this entire revolutionary path of Spiritual life—has been a modification of Conscious Light. Even that Realization, that Knowledge, is a modification of Conscious Light. There is a Conscious Instant in which it becomes Obvious that This Is So. And that is—if one can still apply any name or significance to it whatsoever—most "radical" (or most perfectly "gone-to-the-root") self-understanding.

But the ordinary Yogi, whose Spiritual principle is the search, is involved in fantastic dramas of experience. Such a one has all kinds of things to do—to, with, and around himself or herself—with the body and mind, with all the egoic ornaments, the suffering, the extremes, the endless number of searches, strategies, or egoic works. The ordinary Yogi-ascetic has a fantastic—a fantastically distracting, a fascinating—life! It is a great, great adventure. Even the ordinary Jnani—the philosophical ascetic, one who enjoys conditionally achieved Self-Knowledge—is absorbed in a fascinating life of Silence, of acquired Peace, of strategic Formlessness, separated by a waking sleep. Such a person is absorbed in his or her own inner subjectivity. But for one who has understood, there is no drama. Therefore, I do not have anything with which to fascinate people. No sign, no act, no word, no costume can represent Truth. No closing of the eyes, no blissful smiles, no shuddering, no reports of visions—none of this is necessary to keep My devotees "interested" from day to day. There is not anything that is happening anymore. The only Forceful Communication is That Which cannot be Communicated by any conditional means—neither by purposive silence nor by speech.

Truth does not specially appear in the form of something extraordinary or fascinating. Truth is the most Absolute Communication—and It is the most Obvious Communication, because It is Inherent and Self-Evident. Satsang with Me (or the devotional and Spiritual relationship to Me) is founded in the Inherent and Self-Evident Condition of Reality, and is expressed in the living condition of relationship. Relationship itself always already exists as your living condition. What has to be added in order for that to take place? Not <u>any</u>thing! Your true living condition is expressed in every ordinary or present situation. Relationship itself is, in every moment, always already the case. Therefore, Satsang Itself, the devotional and Spiritual relationship to Me, Reveals the Truth by first Revealing the most obvious of all conditions.

FOURTH FUNDAMENTAL

Ruchira Shaktipat

The Spiritual Gift of the Divine Transmission-Master, Adi Da Samraj

Your Devotional Turning To Me, and My "Bright" Spiritual Self-Transmission In Response To You—These Two, Together, Are The Only-By-Me Revealed and Given Way Of Adidam.

—Avatar Adi Da Samraj
The Dawn Horse Testament Of The Ruchira Avatar

The foundation practice of the Way of Adidam is full when the devotee has firmly established the fundamental practice of Ruchira Avatara Bhakti Yoga and has thoroughly adapted to all the supportive practices (including the life-disciplines, the "conscious process", and "conductivity"). Once this foundation preparation is complete, the devotee has fulfilled the necessary preparation that makes it possible to receive Avatar Adi Da's Gift of His Spiritual Transmission (or Ruchira Shaktipat).

This Gift is Given entirely by the Divine Master Himself—in the course of one or more periods of special Initiatory retreat in His physical Company. This Initiation is Granted by Avatar Adi Da when He is moved to do so, in the case of each individual, by the demonstration of ego-forgetting devotion. He can tell at once if a devotee is ready—if the Yogic signs of equanimity and openness to Him are there.

In addition, the process of Avatar Adi Da's Granting of Spiritual Initiation requires, as an overall context, that the collective gathering of His devotees is fulfilling its responsibility to serve His great purposes in the world.*

Avatar Adi Da has spoken on many occasions of how, traditionally, the Grace of true Shaktipat was rare, given only to the most serious practitioners. Avatar Adi Da's Spiritual Blessing cannot be gained through an ego-based orientation—"If I follow this program of practices, I will 'earn' Shaktipat, and then I will 'have it' from that moment on." Avatar Adi Da's Spiritual Transmission is Him, His Very Person. The circumstance of receiving His Shaktipat is surrender to Him, and not the attempt to "get" something for oneself. One must constantly continue to cultivate the devotional and Spiritual relationship to Him, on the basis of having received His Spiritual Initiation—rather than running away, like a dog with its bone, and presuming to take the Gift of Spiritual Initiation for oneself.

AVATAR ADI DA SAMRAJ: To understand True Shaktipat, the relationship to Transmission-Masters of the past must be studied. Shaktipat is a Transmission-Event. Generally speaking, it is the impulse of the Master that allows it to occur in an individual's case. And that individual must be a suitable vehicle for that Transmission, trusted to the point of maturity. Until that time, there is no True Shaktipat. Preparation for Shaktipat-Transmission involves a psycho-physical transformation of the being. This is because you are armored. Although the Transmission-Master Radiates, that Radiation cannot have a profound effect in the devotee unless the Master makes the gesture. Therefore, there must be a true connection between Master and devotee, based on the true surrender of the devotee.

—February 10, 2002

*Avatar Adi Da has described five key areas (or "Issues") for which the collective gathering of His devotees is responsible: (1) the individual and collective devotional gifts to Avatar Adi Da Samraj of a thriving and rightly adapted culture, community, and mission, (2) providing a Spiritually auspicious Hermitage circumstance for Avatar Adi Da, set-apart from the common world, (3) the perpetuation of the "global ashram", or full interactive culture, of Avatar Adi Da's devotees, (4) honorable and Spiritually sensitive direct service to Avatar Adi Da's bodily (human) Divine Form, and (5) on the basis of true fulfillment of the first four Issues, the process of access to Him for the sake of Spiritual Initiation.

Searchless Beholding of Avatar Adi Da

Being Initiated into Avatar Adi Da's Spiritual Transmission is the most profound transformative event that could ever happen to a human being. His Ruchira Shaktipat opens the being to the unique Spiritual process that He has brought into the world through His Avataric Incarnation. This process is a Divine Yoga, accomplished by Avatar Adi Da in the body-mind of His devotee. And that process continues throughout the entire course of the Way of Adidam—up to the point of receiving His Supreme Gift of Divine Enlightenment, and even beyond that, throughout the process that unfolds (by His Grace) in His Divinely Enlightened devotee.*

When Avatar Adi Da is moved to Grant His Spiritual Initiation, He Installs Himself Spiritually in His devotee. Thus, the devotee is enabled to enter into Spiritual Communion with Him—tangibly experiencing His Love-Blissful Spiritual Presence entering and suffusing the body-mind from Above and Beyond. Everything one has done in the practice until this point is for the purpose of preparing for this sublime Gift.

When this Spiritual Initiation has been Given, one's practice of Ruchira Avatara Bhakti Yoga is transformed. Then the turning of the faculties to Avatar Adi Da opens the being to receive His tangible Spiritual Presence. Ruchira Avatara Bhakti Yoga, engaged as Spiritual Communion with the Divine Avatar, is called "searchless Beholding" of Him—and this searchless Beholding of Him (or Spiritually Activated Ruchira Avatara Bhakti Yoga) becomes the primary form of the practice of Adidam from this point on.

AVATAR ADI DA SAMRAJ: The preparedness to live real Spiritual life in the Way of Adidam is a great matter. The Initiation into searchlessly Beholding Me is the transition beyond the ordinary dimensions of life. It is to enter into the Spiritual domain of existence. It is about entering My Spiritual Sphere. Therefore, it is a profound change of life.

—May 1, 2003

*Avatar Adi Da describes the process of Divine Enlightenment in the Way of Adidam as unfolding in four phases. Please see the description of the "Perfect Practice" and Divine Self-Realization in the following chapter.

Beyond Seeking

Why is this process called searchless Beholding? A fundamental principle of Avatar Adi Da's Wisdom-Teaching is the necessity of understanding and transcending all forms of seeking. Thus, Adidam is specifically not a means of engaging the Spiritual search. That search is to be understood and gone beyond—in always present-time Communion with Avatar Adi Da.

Avatar Adi Da Teaches that seeking is, in fact, the symptom of our activity of self-contraction. It is only on the basis of this self-created unhappiness that we enter into the search. Therefore, along with the fundamental practice of devotional Communion with Avatar Adi Da, you also observe, understand, and transcend the self-contraction, the unconscious activity through which we constantly recreate the sense of a separate, threatened, loveless "self"—seeking for a way to feel "okay" about life.

It is impossible to seek Reality Itself and—as a result of the seeking of It—Find It.

Therefore, you must transcend the search itself.

The only-by-Me Revealed and Given Way of Adidam Is the One and Only (and, altogether, Divine) Way (and Real practice) of understanding and transcending the search for Truth, the search for Reality Itself, the search for Real God, the search for Happiness (or Self-Evidently Divine Love-Bliss) Itself, and (indeed) all seeking—by directly (and constantly) transcending "search" (and the egoic cause of seeking) itself.

The only-by-Me Revealed and Given Way of Adidam is not a way (or means) for seeking Truth, or Reality, or Real God, or Happiness—or for achieving Truth, or Reality, or Real God, or Happiness as a result of that search.

The only-by-Me Revealed and Given Way of Adidam is the Way (and, therefore, the active—and, necessarily, ego-transcending—practice) of the always present-time devotional (or Me-recognizing, and to-Me-responding) Realization of Love-Bliss—Which Is Happiness, Truth, Reality, and the only Real God.

—Avatar Adi Da Samraj
Da Love-Ananda Gita

What makes Adidam a non-seeking Way is that Avatar Adi Da has Appeared in the world, as the bodily Manifested Revelation of the Divine Reality. By means of the practice of devotion to Him in His bodily human Divine Form, you are Given always present-time access to Love-Blissful Communion with Him, and thus with Reality Itself, or Truth Itself. Truth Itself is Realized to be not "elsewhere", not to be sought and found only in the future. Seeking itself is transcended in the always present "finding" of Truth in relationship to Avatar Adi Da Samraj.

Likewise, the description "searchless Beholding" indicates that even Avatar Adi Da's Spiritual Initiation is not something one should seek. Such Initiation is Given by Him in its right time, in the context of the relationship between Him and His devotee.

Avatar Adi Da's "Tangible Touch" —and Spiritual "Intoxication"

I Am the Divine Love-Bliss, Coming from Infinitely Above, and Surrounding the body, and Entering it, Infusing it, Pervading it—Distracting you from self-attention and Turning your attention to Me. Feeling Me, breathing Me. Living in Me, Lived by Me. And My Characteristic is Love-Bliss Itself, whatever other sensations there may be in the body-mind itself.

Spiritual Communion with Me is of this nature.

—Avatar Adi Da Samraj
Ruchira Shaktipat Yoga

The principal events of any period of Initiatory retreat are the times of silently Beholding Avatar Adi Da's physical human Form, in a hall specially reserved for this purpose.* In such occasions of silent Beholding—and also in any other circumstance, whenever He may be moved to Give the Gift of His Spiritual Transmission—Avatar Adi Da's Ruchira Shaktipat can be felt as a tangible Touch that manifests in different ways according to the individual. Most often, devotees first feel Avatar Adi Da's Spiritual Transmission as a pressure at the crown of the head, followed by the descent of His Blissful Spiritual Force into the body-mind. There is no one way for His Spiritual Transmission to manifest—but, typically, the experience of Avatar Adi Da's Ruchira Shaktipat registers gradually, like a process of "saturation". He has described that, just as a sponge expands and fills as it slowly soaks up water, the body-mind is gradually filled and permeated by His Divine Spiritual Transmission.

As the body-mind goes through the process of adapting to Avatar Adi Da's Spirit-Force, various purifying experiences may occur in body, emotion, mind, and breath. Such experiences are called "kriyas". The body may move or shake in various spontaneous

*After Avatar Adi Da's physical Lifetime, the function of Spiritual Initiation on formal retreats will be perpetuated by the collective body of the Ruchira Sannyasin Order (see p. 21), in the Hermitage Ashram circumstances Spiritually Empowered by Avatar Adi Da during His physical Lifetime.

ways, even at times taking on unfamiliar Yogic postures. There may be intense heart-feeling and emotional release through weeping or sudden vocalization. Mind and thought may become a speechless stillness, with attention deeply established in Avatar Adi Da's Divine Love-Bliss. And the breath may go through all sorts of changes—becoming exaggeratedly rapid, or (otherwise) becoming deeply relaxed, and even spontaneously suspended for periods of time.

At times, receiving Avatar Adi Da's Divine Spiritual Transmission can also take the form of an overwhelming Spiritual "Intoxication", or the feeling of a forceful Infusion of His Divine Spirit-Force. However, extraordinary experiences in themselves are not the goal of practice in the Way of Adidam. Rather, they are simply phenomena that may occur spontaneously. It is the process of devotional and Spiritual Communion with Him, developing more and more over time—sometimes showing extraordinary signs, sometimes not—that grows and deepens the devotee's practice of searchless Beholding of Him.

The Way I have Revealed and Given is not any form of seeking.

The Way I have Revealed and Given is, most fundamentally, a matter of merely Beholding Me.

To merely Behold Me is to be constantly engaged in devotional resort to Me.

*Merely Beholding Me is the fundamental (and always primary) practice of the only-by-Me Revealed and Given Way of Adidam Ruchiradam.**

The Way of Adidam Ruchiradam is searchless Beholding of Me, without self-reference or strategic self-manipulation, and (altogether) such that My Avataric Divine Spiritual Blessing is effortlessly and tangibly experienced. . . .

Searchless Beholding of Me is a Spiritual matter.

Searchless Beholding of Me allows you to receive My Avataric

* "Adidam Ruchiradam" is a fuller form of reference to the Way of Adidam. The word "Ruchiradam" (coined by Avatar Adi Da) indicates that Adidam is the Way of most perfectly Realizing the "Bright".

Divine Gift of whole bodily (or total psycho-physical) reception of the Self-Existing and Self-Radiant Divine Conscious Light of My Own Spiritually Self-"Bright" Person.

Ruchira Shaktipat . . . is the Process (or Mechanism) by Which I Spiritually Transmit My Divine Conscious Light into the conditionally manifested realms.

Thus, fully established practice of the Way of Adidam Ruchiradam is, altogether, a practice engaged within My Ruchira Shaktipat Circumstance.

Adidam Ruchiradam is not a technique, but a relationship.

Adidam Ruchiradam is a relationship (to Me) in which I Spiritually Transmit Myself to you, and you receive (and respond to) My Avataric Divine Spiritual Self-Transmission (or Ruchira Shaktipat).

Adidam Ruchiradam is searchless Beholding of Me.

Searchless Beholding of Me is the Essence of Satsang with Me.

Searchless Beholding of Me is heart-recognition of Me.

Searchless Beholding of Me is the fully developed Essence of Ruchira Avatara Bhakti Yoga.

Searchless Beholding of Me is participation in My Avataric Divine Spiritual Self-Transmission.

—Avatar Adi Da Samraj
"No Seeking / Mere Beholding"

Once a devotee has been Spiritually Initiated by Avatar Adi Da into the practice of searchlessly Beholding Him, the individual engages further periods of retreat in Avatar Adi Da's physical Company as frequently as possible—as a principal means of deepening his or her devotional and (now) Spiritual relationship to Avatar Adi Da Samraj, and (at certain further points in the Spiritual process) as a further essential process of Initiation by Avatar Adi Da into more mature stages of practice.

A "Law of Vibration"

In the following passage from *The Dawn Horse Testament*, Avatar Adi Da uses the metaphor of two tuning forks sympathetically vibrating with each other to further illustrate the process that occurs in the searchless Beholding of Him.

Access To My Avataric Physical Human Company (or, After My Avataric Physical Human Lifetime, To The physical human Company and By-Me-Spiritually-Empowered Circumstances Of My Instrumental "Ruchira Sannyasin" Devotees) Is A Unique Divine Spiritual Gift, Which Is Effective (In Transforming The Totality Of The Four psycho-physical Faculties Of My Any Rightly Prepared Devotee) By Virtue Of A Simple "Law Of Vibration".

If You Consistently Turn The psycho-physical Faculties To Me, You Are (Thus and Thereby—By Surrendering, Forgetting, and Transcending the ego-"I") Sympathetically Attuned To Me. If a tuning fork Is Struck (or, Thereby, or Otherwise, Caused To Vibrate At its Characteristic Frequency), and Then a Second tuning fork (Of Similar Structure, Capable Of Resonating With the First) Is Brought Into Promixity With the First tuning fork, the Second tuning fork (Even If it Is Not Already Vibrating, and Not, Otherwise, Struck) Will Begin To Vibrate Sympathetically (or "In Sympathy" With the First tuning fork). I Am Like the (First) Vibrating tuning fork—and You (As My Rightly Prepared Devotee) Are Like the (Second) Non-Vibrating tuning fork that Begins To Vibrate By Coming Into Proximity With the Already Vibrating tuning fork. Thus, By Coming Into True Sympathetic Association With Me, You Begin To Vibrate "In Sympathy" With Me—Until (In Due Course) You Become Completely Resonant With Me.

The Process Of Access To My Avataric Physical Human Company (or, After My Avataric Physical Human Lifetime, To The physical human Company and By-Me-Spiritually-Empowered Circumstances Of My Instrumental "Ruchira Sannyasin" Devotees) Is, Literally, A Vibratory Matter, Exactly Of The Nature I Have Just Described. If You Are (Thus) Vibrating With (and Attuned To) Me, You Become (Progressively More and More Deeply) Aware Of The

Pressure (and The Fullness) Of My Avatarically Self-Transmitted Divine Spiritual Presence. You Begin To Notice Certain Characteristic Signs Of The Spiritual Reception (and Awareness) Of Me—Including A Tangible bodily Vibration (or In-Filling Feeling Of Saturation With Energy) and A Characteristic "Thickness" Of the breath. Altogether, This Process Of Deepening Spiritual Sensitivity To Me Can Be Likened To The Process Of a sponge Gradually Soaking Up (and Swelling With) water. As You Are Given Over In That Sympathetic Attunement To Me, There Is, Over time, A (By-My-Avataric-Divine-Spiritual-Grace-Given) Purification Of Your Total psycho-physical ego-Patterning, Potentially (and Even Soon, or Rather Immediately) Signed By The Spontaneous Purifying Occurrence Of kriyas, and mudras, and pranayama (or automatic slow or rapid Yogic breathing-"Conductivity"), and other psycho-physical (or bodily, emotional, mental, and breath-pattern) phenomenon of all kinds (As the body-mind Requires and Allows). Such Are The First (and Progressively Deepening) "Symptoms" Of The Process Of Becoming Spiritually Attuned To Me.

If You (As My Foundationally Fully Prepared Devotee) Come Into My Avataric Physical Human Company (or, After My Avataric Physical Human Lifetime, Into The physical human Company and By-Me-Spiritually-Empowered Circumstances Of My Instrumental "Ruchira Sannyasin" Devotees) and Do Not Demonstrate <u>Any</u> Signs Of Spiritually Receiving Me, This Simply Indicates That You Are Not (In present time) Sympathetically Attuned To Me (but, Rather, Are psycho-physically self-Contracted, and, Thus and Thereby, Dissociated From Me). In That Case, You Are, In Effect, Holding the Two tines of the tuning fork With Your hand—Thereby Preventing The Possibility Of Sympathetic Vibration. Such Is the effect Of The self-Contraction-Act That Is the ego.

The Only-By-Me Revealed and Given Way Of Adidam Is The Devotional Turning Of The psycho-physical Faculties To Me—Bringing The Faculties Into Sympathetic Association With Me, Such That You Are Vibrated Whole bodily (or As A psycho-physical Totality) By My Vibration (and This, Ultimately, and In Due Course, To The Most Perfect Degree Of Complete Attunement With Me). If You Take Your hand Off the tines of the tuning fork, the tuning fork (or Your body-mind itself) Will (Inevitably) Vibrate Sympathetically With Me. Therefore, Always Turn To Me In My Avatarically-Born Bodily (Human) Divine Form—and (Thereby) Become Sympathetically Attuned To Me. And, When You (As My Foundationally Fully Prepared Devotee) Begin To (As Often As Possible) Come Into My Avataric Physical Human Company (or, After My Avataric Physical Human Lifetime, Into The physical human Company and By-Me-Spiritually-Empowered Circumstances Of My Instrumental "Ruchira Sannyasin" Devotees)—Allow My Avataric Divine Spiritual Self-Transmission To Vibrate You.

If the tuning fork that is Your body-mind Is Vibrated By Me, I Can (Progressively, and In Due Course) Make it Vibrate To The Degree Of Absolute Intensity. But If You Are Gripping the tines of the tuning fork, I Cannot Do My Avataric Divine Spiritual Work With You.

Therefore, Take Your hand Off the tines—and Come To Me.
Be Always Attuned To Me—and Vibrated By Me.
I Vibrate You By Merely Being.
Therefore, You Must Come To Me To Merely Be With Me.

—Avatar Adi Da Samraj
The Dawn Horse Testament Of The Ruchira Avatar

The primary practice of searchlessly Beholding Avatar Adi Da, established by His direct Spiritual Initiation, is an incredible Grace. Through that Initiation, human beings experience and participate in the truly Spiritual process, in relationship to Him. This is the Fourth Fundamental of the True World-Religion of Adidam. ■

Surrender to the Divine Source as a Tangible Person

AVATAR ADI DA SAMRAJ: Once the primary practice of searchlessly Beholding Me begins, it always continues. The context in which it is done develops over time, but the primary practice is always primary. It is always fundamental to this Way of devotional and Spiritual relationship with Me. The practices of the "conscious process" and "conductivity" are also always done, but they are developed (or elaborated) in response to this always primary practice.

The primary practice of searchlessly Beholding Me, the responsive "conscious process", and responsive "conductivity" practice are all developed on the foundation of the fundamental disciplines and responsibility of Ruchira Avatara Bhakti Yoga, together with all the life-disciplines of the Way of Adidam. The Way of Adidam develops as an elaboration of these basics, which are established at the beginning. The Way of Adidam itself is the devotional and Spiritual relationship to Me, or searchless Beholding of Me, which begins as soon as the period of foundation preparatory practice is complete.

The Way of Adidam is based on access to Me and Invocation of Me. Fundamental to that access and that Invocation is My Avataric Divine Spiritual Transmission-Work, My Ruchira-Shaktipat-Work. The process of Ruchira Avatara Bhakti Yoga is progressive. Its foundation dimension is devotion to Me through the turning of the four faculties to Me. This becomes the foundation for the primary practice of searchlessly Beholding Me. That primary practice is simply a development of the foundation practice of Ruchira Avatara Bhakti Yoga. When it is established in the context of the responsibilities I have Described, and on the basis of the Spiritual Initiation Given by Me, the approach to Me in the manner of searchless Beholding is a natural and inevitable development (or extension) of the foundation practice of Ruchira Avatara Bhakti Yoga.

Searchless Beholding of Me is not based on any kind of seeking from a place within the body or the mind. It occurs spontaneously. My Avataric Divine Spiritual Transmission Causes it.

Therefore, all of the descriptions of the fully established Way of Adidam are descriptions of a process that occurs in real devotional and Spiritual Communion with Me. The signs of that process come from My Avataric Divine Spiritual Transmission. That process develops via (more and more) effectively ego-transcending Communion with Me, such that I Demonstrate My Avatarically Self-Transmitted Divine Spiritual Presence in your body-mind through various signs.

My summary Word describes (or accounts for) a Spiritual process Given by Me. That process is not merely a philosophically-based technique of seeking. It has nothing to do with such seeking.

The original disposition of My devotee is simply one of movement toward Me—the devotional recognition-response to Me, the faculties moved toward Me. You begin by embracing the disciplines according to My Instruction. In due course, you begin to Behold Me in this searchless manner, and I Demonstrate Myself Spiritually in your whole bodily experience.

You do not "do" anything Spiritually. You experience Me tangibly, Spiritually—and that experience of Me is purifying and transformative. It shows various signs. And when those transformations appear, the process advances.

The Way of Adidam has unique characteristics, and they are all based on My tangible Spiritual Transmission of Divine Grace. They are not based on philosophy or thinking or techniques. The entire process in My Company is based on the devotional and (in due course) Spiritual relationship to Me, and not on any technique of seeking.

If you want to know that this process in My Company is true, then experience Me. That is all. It is not about believing something or merely thinking that it is so. It is a matter of approaching Me as a devotee, in the searchlessly Me-Beholding manner of true devotion.

For the devotee, that is sufficient. In the context of My devotee's searchless Beholding of Me, I Reveal Myself to him or her through various signs. The Way of Adidam is simply the process of My devotee being given over to Me, combined with Me. Altogether, the Way of Adidam is the process of manifested conditions being given over to their Source. That is it—being surrendered in the Divine Source. Not the "Divine Source" as a philosophical principle or an abstract idea, but as a tangible Person here, Avatarically Self-Manifested, Speaking to you now.

—August 16, 2002

Fifth Fundamental

Ruchira Shaktipat Yoga

The Spiritually Awakened Practice of Adidam and the Ultimate Process of Divine Enlightenment

The only Way to Realize Real God is to Commune with Real God, to receive Real God. How could it be otherwise? If you are ego-bound, ego-possessed, self-contracted—you can look and seek in every direction (through the structure of the body-mind), but you will never (by means of such efforts) truly Find The One Who Is Always Already The Case. These lookings and searches are the conventional efforts, the evolutionary ego-efforts, of mankind.

The Great Process comes about when the Divine Intervenes, Appears, Incarnates, Blesses, Teaches the understanding and the transcending of ego—such that the direct Divine Blessing may be received and the Great Divine Yoga may be entered into. This is What I Do.

It is so. The Divine must Intervene. That is why I Am here—for this Great and Spiritual Process and Purpose.

—Avatar Adi Da Samraj
Ruchira Shaktipat Yoga

The Fifth Fundamental of the True World-Religion of Adidam is the process that unfolds on the basis of the fully established devotional and Spiritual relationship with Avatar Adi Da. It is a unique process (or Yoga), because of the unique Avataric nature of Adi Da's Divine Spiritual Transmission ("Shaktipat") of the "Bright" ("Ruchira").

The Divine Is Above and Prior— but You Don't Have to Go "Up" or "Within" in Order to "Get There"

In the world's highest Spiritual traditions, there have been two characteristic approaches to attainment or enlightenment. One is the effort to "go up" and the other is the effort to "go within".

In the traditions of ascent, Spiritual practice has often been likened to climbing a ladder—a progress from "lower" to "higher". Some see this ladder primarily as a matter of going "higher" by becoming more and more "pure". Others (especially in the tradition of Kundalini Yoga) see the body itself as "containing" the ladder. The fundamental energy of life is presumed to lie at the base of the spine, and the aspirant engages practices that are intended to "raise" that energy up through the spine, eventually reaching the crown of the head (and going even beyond the crown of the head). This is held to be the method of attaining Union with the Divine.

In the traditions of interiorization, Spiritual practice has been described as a process of coming to Stand as the True Self, by intentionally excluding awareness of the conditional world—a progress to the presumed "inner essence" of one's being. Some traditions (such as certain schools of Buddhism) see this interiorization as a way of locating the Nirvanic "Void" of no-desire. Other traditions (such as Advaitism) see this interiorization as a way of Abiding as the Divine Self.

Adidam stands in contrast to all such approaches. The Way of Adidam does not require any effort either of "going up" or of "going within". Indeed, in the Way of Adidam, all such efforts must be inspected, understood, and gone beyond. Whatever real impulse to Realize the Divine may be involved in such efforts, one of Avatar Adi Da's core Revelations is that all such efforts are inevitably involved with ego—either the ego-search for the bliss of subtle experience (achieved by "going up") or the ego-search for the bliss of no-experience (achieved by "going within").

In the Way of Adidam, Spiritual Realization is a Gift freely Given by Avatar Adi Da Samraj. Avatar Adi Da's Divine Spiritual Transmission Enters the conditional world from Above and Beyond, Infusing and Transforming all that appears. This is why Adidam is not a form of self-effort. There is no necessity to "climb the ladder" or "go inside" in order to "get to" the Divine. In fact, you cannot "get to" the Divine by any effort of your own. You can only receive the Divine—by responding to Avatar Adi Da's Spiritual Attractiveness and relinquishing all forms of ego-effort and ego-activity.

Only the Way of Adidam is the Divine Gift of directly and fully receiving the Blessing-Transmission of Real God, from His Divine Self-Domain Infinitely Above and Most Prior—even in the midst of the world.

AVATAR ADI DA SAMRAJ: My Avataric Divine Self-Revelation is a unique Revelation for the sake of beings, because It is the Revelation of That Which Is Prior and Divine, and not merely a description of how to "get back" to the Divine by seeking. Thus, My Spiritual Transmission is the Transmission of That Which Is Prior and Divine. My Spiritual Transmission does not originate below, or in the outer conditions of conditional existence. My Spiritual Transmission is Given from Beyond and Prior and Above.

You are Given the direct Revelation of That Which Is Prior and Above. That Is My Spiritual Transmission. It is not an energy that moves you toward What Is Above and Prior. It is the Spirit-Force of That Which Is Always Already Above and Prior. Therefore, to receive Me is to receive that Unique Divine Revelation and to be Purified and Grown by heart-Communion with Me—That Which Is Divine, and Priorly Ascended, and Infinitely Beyond (and Prior to) all conditions.

My Transmitted Spiritual Divine Presence Purifies and Affects all the conditions of existence, but It does not originate from below and outside. Therefore, the process and practice of heart-Communion with Me is not an egoic effort generated from below and moving toward Above by a process of seeking. It is a totally different kind of process, which involves the always immediate transcending of egoity itself—the principle of egoity, the activity of egoity, the method of egoity. That is specifically transcended in the practice of Adidam.

Adidam is not a practice that leads toward eventual egolessness Above and Beyond. When it is truly lived, Adidam is an inherently ego-transcending practice. In other words, the sadhana is not ego-based. It is not that devotees of Mine—simply because they are devotees of Mine—are egoless. It is that the sadhana is not based on the method of egoity or the position of egoity or the bound condition of egoity. Rather, the practice is based on the devotional response to Me, the turning of the principal faculties to Me. Therefore, the practice of Adidam is Communion with Me—That Which Is Infinitely Ascended, Prior, Divine, Beyond—allowing My Spiritually Self-Transmitted Person and Presence, the "Bright" Itself, to Purify and Transform the conditions of existence, the conditions of apparent egoity. It is a constant process of ego-transcendence, of ego-surrender, of transcending the activity, disposition, and method of egoity itself. Therefore, it is a unique process.

The Way of Adidam does not develop by a gross effort relative to egoity. It is by a straightforward process of surrender into heart-Communion with Me—simply turning to Me, receiving My Infusion of the "Bright" Itself, the Divine Spiritual Self-Condition Itself, and allowing My Infusion to Purify the being (starting from the subtlest of the subtle levels and moving from thence toward the gross levels of existence)—that it becomes transformative and shows unique signs.

—April 17, 2003

The Seven Stages of Life

One of Avatar Adi Da's unique Gifts to humanity is His precise "mapping" of the potential developmental course of human experience as it unfolds through the gross, subtle, and causal dimensions of the being. He describes this course in terms of six stages of life—which account for, and correspond to, all possible orientations to religion and culture that have arisen in human history. His own Avataric Revelation—the Realization of the "Bright", Prior to all experience—is the seventh stage of life. Understanding this structure of seven stages illuminates the unique nature of the process of Adidam.

The first three (or foundation) stages of life constitute the ordinary course of human adaptation—characterized (respectively) by bodily, emotional, and mental growth. Each of the first three stages of life takes approximately seven years to be established. Every individual who lives to an adult age inevitably adapts (although, generally speaking, only partially) to the first three stages of life. In the general case, this is where the developmental process stops—at the gross level of adaptation. Religions based fundamentally on beliefs and moral codes (without direct experience of the dimensions beyond the material world) belong to this foundation level of human development.

The fourth stage of life is characterized by a deep impulse to Communion with the Divine. It is in the context of the fourth stage of life (when one is no longer wedded to the purposes of the first three stages of life) that the true Spiritual process can begin. In the history of the Great Tradition, those involved in the process of the fourth stage of life have characteristically felt the Divine to be a great "Other", in Whom they aspired to become absorbed, through devotional love and service. However, in the Way of Adidam, the presumption that the Divine is "Other" is transcended from the beginning.

In the Way of Adidam, the process of the first three stages of life is lived on the basis of the devotional heart-impulse that is otherwise characteristic of the fourth stage of life. No matter what the age of the individual who comes to Avatar Adi Da, there will generally be signs of failed adaptation to the first three stages of life. But the practice is not a matter of attempting to overcome such failed adaptation through one's own (inevitably egoic) effort or struggle. Rather, the practice is to turn the faculties to Avatar Adi Da in devotional surrender. In that manner, the virtue of the fourth stage of life—the devotional heart-impulse to Commune with the Divine—is specifically animated from the beginning, in living response to Avatar Adi Da. Thus, whatever must be done to righten the first three stages of life occurs in the devotional context of heart-Communion with Him.

Avatar Adi Da has Revealed that the true Spiritual process, beginning in the context of the fourth stage of life, involves two great dimensions—which He calls the "vertical" and the "horizontal".

The descending aspect of the vertical process characterizes the fourth stage of life, while the ascending aspect characterizes the fifth stage of life. (Please see "The Esoteric Anatomy of the Spiritual Process: 'Vertical' and 'Horizontal' Dimensions of the Being", pp. 133-137.) As it has been known in the history of the Great Tradition, the fifth stage process is the ascent toward absorption into the Divine Matrix of Light Infinitely Above, thereby (ultimately) Realizing the Divine as Light (or Energy) Itself. (Although this Realization is a true "taste" of the Very Divine Condition, It is achieved by means of the conditional effort of ascent—and, therefore, the Realization Itself is also conditional, or non-permanent.) The fifth stage of life is the ultimate process associated with the subtle dimension of existence.

The horizontal process characterizes the sixth stage of life. As it has been known in the history of the Great Tradition, the sixth stage process is the exclusion of all awareness of the "outside" world (in both its gross and subtle dimensions), by "secluding" oneself within the heart—in order to rest in the Divine Self, Realized (ultimately) as Consciousness Itself. (Like the ultimate Realization associated with the fifth stage of life, the sixth stage Realization is also a true "taste" of the Very Divine Condition. However, It is also achieved by conditional means—the conditional effort of exclusion—and, therefore, the Realization Itself is also conditional, or non-permanent.) The sixth stage of life is the process associated with the causal dimension of existence.

As Avatar Adi Da has pointed out, even though the fifth stage and sixth stage processes are, in fact, stages in the single process that culminates in Divine Enlightenment (or the seventh stage Realization uniquely Given by Him), the typical traditional view has been that the two processes are <u>alternative</u> approaches to Spiritual Realization. Indeed, these approaches (of either going "Up" or going "Deep") have usually been regarded to be incompatible with each other.

In the Way of Adidam, the "Perfect Practice" encompasses <u>both</u> the vertical process (otherwise characteristically associated with the fifth stage of life) <u>and</u> the horizontal process (otherwise characteristically associated with the sixth stage of life). Thus, in the Way of Adidam, there is no "preference" exercised in favor of either the "Upward" process or the "Inward" process—either the Realization of the Divine as Light Itself or the Realization of the Divine as Consciousness Itself. In the Way of Adidam, both the ultimate "Upward" Realization and the ultimate "Inward"

Realization are Freely Given by Avatar Adi Da to the rightly prepared and rightly practicing devotee. No effort—either of ascent or of exclusion—is required. And, in fact, all such effort must be inspected, understood, and transcended.

This unique and unprecedented orientation to the developmental processes of the fifth and the sixth stages of life is made possible by the full reception of Avatar Adi Da's Gift of Divine Spiritual Transmission. When the devotee (in the context of the fourth stage of life in the Way of Adidam) is fully open to Avatar Adi Da's Spiritual Transmission, His Spiritual Descent of the "Thumbs" takes over the body-mind, showing specific Yogic signs. In this "Samadhi of the 'Thumbs'", there is a profound turnabout in one's awareness of Him. While still always turning to Him devotionally in His bodily (human) Form, one begins to recognize Him, Spiritually, as Consciousness Itself—the Root-Position of existence, Prior to all that is arising in body, mind, and world. This recognition is Spiritually established—and it is the basis for making the transition to the "Perfect Practice". It is a profound shift, away from identification with the body-mind. From this point on, Avatar Adi Da's Revelation of His own Condition of Consciousness Itself becomes the Position in which one Stands, and from that Position the phenomena associated with both the fifth stage of life and the sixth stage of life will arise. In the "Perfect Practice", one is no longer practicing from the point of view of the body-mind and its faculties. Now, devotional turning to Him (or Ruchira Avatara Bhakti Yoga) takes the form of simply "choosing" to Stand in His Position (rather than the ego-position)—inspecting and feeling beyond the root-tendency to contract and create the self-identity called "I".

The seventh stage of life, or the Realization of Avatar Adi Da's own "Bright" Divine Self-Condition, transcends the entire course of human potential. In the seventh stage of life, the impulse to Realize the Divine (as Light) by going

"Up" and the impulse to Realize the Divine (as Consciousness) by going "Deep" are (by Avatar Adi Da's Divine Grace) simultaneously fulfilled. In that fulfillment, Avatar Adi Da Samraj Himself is most perfectly Realized. He is Realized as the "Bright", the Single Divine Unity of Consciousness and Energy—or Conscious Light Itself. This unique Realization, or Divine Enlightenment, wipes away every trace of dissociation from the body-mind and the world. There is no impulse to seek or to avoid any experience. Rather, everything that arises is Divinely Self-Recognized to be merely a modification of the Conscious Light of Reality Itself.

The seventh stage Realization is absolutely Unconditional. It does not depend on any form of effort by the individual. Rather, It is a Divine Gift, Given by Avatar Adi Da to the devotee who has utterly surrendered all egoity to Him. Therefore, the seventh stage Realization is permanent.

Altogether, the Way of Adidam is not about dwelling in any of the potential experiences of the first six stages of life. The Way of Adidam is about transcending the entire structure of the human being and of the conditional reality—gross, subtle, and causal. Therefore, the Way of Adidam transcends both the urge to "have" experiences and the urge to "exclude" experience. The Way of Adidam is based, from the beginning, on the Divine Avatar's "Bright" State, which is Realized progressively (and, ultimately, most perfectly), by means of His Divine Spiritual Descent in the body-mind of His devotee.

Listening, Hearing, Seeing, and the "Perfect Practice": The Unfolding Signs of Awakening in the Way of Adidam

As an unfolding process, Adidam develops through four distinct phases:

- listening
- hearing
- seeing
- the "Perfect Practice"

This is a progressive process based on growing devotional heart-recognition of, and heart-response to, Avatar Adi Da, and on His Spiritual Initiation of the devotee into more and more profound dimensions of the Way in His Company. The phases of this process are not goals to be attained, nor are they directly correlated with the stages of life as demonstrated in the history of the Great Tradition. Rather, these four phases are simply the unfolding signs of a life lived as always present-time heart-Communion with Avatar Adi Da, cultivating the unique and direct relationship with Him.

Listening

"Listening" is Avatar Adi Da's technical term for the beginning practice of the Way of Adidam. A listening devotee literally "listens" to Avatar Adi Da's Instruction and applies it in his or her life. The listening process includes the original student-beginner adaptation to (1) the fundamental practice of Ruchira Avatara Bhakti Yoga, (2) the supportive life-disciplines, and (3) the responsive practices of the "conscious process" and "conductivity". It also includes a period of demonstration of the true balance of the being that comes with the establishment of the devotional Yoga of turning the faculties to Avatar Adi Da Samraj.

Upon receiving Avatar Adi Da's direct Spiritual Initiation into searchless Beholding of Him, the practice of listening becomes greatly intensified and concentrated. In real Spiritual Communion with Avatar Adi Da, the awareness of the habitual act of self-contraction as that which is preventing such Communion with Him becomes magnified. You spontaneously observe in every moment that you are tending to turn away from Avatar Adi Da. Then you are naturally turned to Him, thus relinquishing the separative activity of the self-contraction.

Hearing

As this (now Spiritually Activated) listening process unfolds by the Grace of Avatar Adi Da's Spiritual Transmission, a profound crisis in conscious awareness is provoked. You come to the point of the undeniable understanding that the self-contraction is the fundamental activity that creates the sense of separate self. You directly hear Avatar Adi Da's Argument for yourself. What previously tended to be an automaticity now becomes a matter for which you can consistently be responsible. The self-contraction is seen to be unnecessary, and you are able to consistently relinquish that activity and the effort of struggle against it. You are awakened to a capability for love and free feeling in every kind of circumstance, and you discover that no circumstance in your life is an impediment to devotional and Spiritual Communion with Avatar Adi Da.

Seeing

As you persist in the demonstration of hearing, a Spiritual conversion occurs, by Avatar Adi Da's Grace. You have already been Awakened to the process of receiving Avatar Adi Da's Spiritual Transmission, in the listening stage. With the advent of seeing, you become fully responsible for receiving His Spirit-Force in every moment, based on the hearing-capability of transcending the activity of self-contraction. It becomes obvious, in your living experience, that everything arising, including your own body-mind, is arising in a field of Spirit-Energy, Avatar Adi Da's

Spiritual "Brightness". His Spiritual Presence is identified with the same degree of clarity as His bodily (human) Form (although feeling-Contemplation of His bodily human Form always remains the devotional foundation of the practice, even once you have become profoundly sensitive to His Spiritual Presence). With seeing comes the spontaneous awakening of deep, Spiritually responsive love.

Throughout all the phases of Spiritually Awakened practice (starting with the first period of special Initiatory retreat), retreats in Avatar Adi Da's physical Company are engaged as frequently as possible—as a most potent means of deepening and quickening the Spiritual process He Activates in His devotees. (Special Initiatory retreats occur at certain times of transition in practice, while retreats in general can occur at any time for Spiritually Awakened devotees.) When the signs of the profound Spiritual transformation of the seeing process begin to appear, you (necessarily) apply for a second period of special Initiatory retreat in Avatar Adi Da's physical Company. On this particular retreat, He Initiates you (when He is moved to do so by your Spiritual responsiveness to Him and your demonstrated readiness for this transition) into a more advanced dimension of searchlessly Beholding Him. Through His Initiatory Blessing, you more and more allow yourself to open upwardly to Him—such that body, emotion, mind, and breath are "Melted" by His down-Flowing Spiritual Infusion.

As the process of seeing develops, your body-mind becomes more and more sublimed by Avatar Adi Da's Spirit-Baptism, purified of any patterns that diminish that reception. You experience Avatar Adi Da's Transmission of the "Bright" in the unique form that He describes as the "experience of the 'Thumbs'", culminating in the "Samadhi of the 'Thumbs'"—and, through this process, you are gracefully grown entirely beyond identification with the body-mind. This is a Gift of Spiritual Awakening as the Witness-Consciousness that stands prior to body, mind, and world, and even the act of attention itself. This Awakening to the Witness-Consciousness indicates that it is time for a third period of special Initiatory retreat in Avatar Adi Da's physical Company, in which (when He is moved to do so by your Spiritual responsiveness to Him and your demonstrated readiness for this transition) He Spiritually Initiates you into the "Perfect Practice".

The Esoteric Anatomy of the Spiritual Process: "Vertical" and "Horizontal" Dimensions of the Being

One of the unique aspects of Avatar Adi Da's Revelation of the Way of Adidam is His complete description of the esoteric anatomy of the human being and how this relates to the Spiritual process. Just as the human body has a gross anatomy (of bones, flesh, nerves, and so on), there is also an esoteric anatomy, consisting of three primary structures. The esoteric anatomy of the human body-mind is the basis for all dimensions of human experience—of the ordinary, extraordinary, mystical, and Transcendental kind. Understanding this esoteric anatomy is a key to understanding what makes the Way of Adidam uniquely complete, and why the Divine Enlightenment that Avatar Adi Da Offers is an unprecedented Gift.

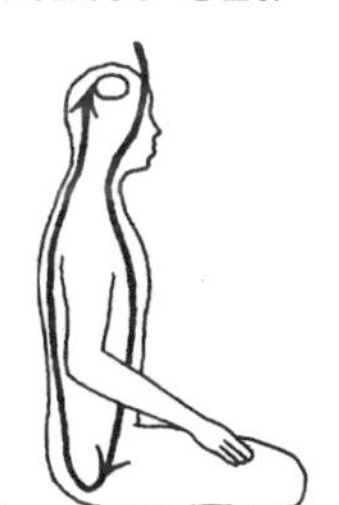

The first structure of esoteric anatomy is what Avatar Adi Da calls "the Circle". The Circle is a pathway through the body, composed of two arcs. The descending arc (or "frontal line") starts at the crown of the head and goes downwards to the perineum. The ascending arc (or "spinal line") starts at the perineum and goes upwards to the crown of the head. The Circle is the primary energy-pathway in the body, through which both the natural energy of life and the Divine Spirit-Energy flow. As you become more sensitive to the subtle dimensions of experience, you become capable of feeling energy moving in your body through the Circle.

The Spiritual Initiation that Avatar Adi Da Gives to His fully prepared listening devotees is the Infusion of His

Divine Spirit-Energy (or Spirit-Current) into the frontal line of the Circle. As you mature in the practice of Adidam, the Circle becomes more and more tangibly full of Avatar Adi Da's Divine Spirit-Current—first in the frontal line, and then also in the spinal line. On certain occasions in the practice of a Spiritually mature devotee, the entire Circle will become utterly full of His Divine Spirit-Current—so open to His Divine Infusion that one ceases to be identified with body or mind in the usual sense, and becomes aware (instead) of existing as a vastly expanded spherical form of the Divine "Brightness". This is the Samadhi of the "Thumbs"—a form of Samadhi uniquely Given by Avatar Adi Da. Eventually, the experience of the "Thumbs" becomes constant, such that the presumption of existing as body and mind no longer "rules" one's life. Then one is ready to receive Avatar Adi Da's Gift of the Awakening to the Witness-Consciousness, which makes possible the beginning of the "Perfect Practice".

Because there is a "downward-and-upward" quality to the Circle (with its descending and ascending arcs), Avatar Adi Da refers to the Circle as the "vertical" dimension of esoteric anatomy. Most of the world's Spiritual traditions are focused in processes that relate to the Circle—seeking, as an ultimate result, some kind of "ascended" Union with the Divine (found by subtly ascending beyond the body-mind, via ascent through and beyond the crown of the head). In the most advanced traditional developments of this "vertical" approach to the Divine, there is, in fact, ascent to the Source-Matrix of Divine Light which is infinitely above. Such ascended Union with the Divine, however, is not permanent (or eternal), because it depends on the effort of the individual—the effort to "go up". Thus, such ascended Union with the Divine is not most perfect Divine Enlightenment. Rather, it is a matter of "choosing" the "Light" (or "Energy") aspect of the Divine—over the "Consciousness" aspect.

The second structure of esoteric anatomy is what Avatar Adi Da calls "the three stations of the heart". The three "stations" are:

The "left side"—corresponding to the physical heart, and the gross dimension of the being

The "middle station"—corresponding to the "heart chakra" (or "anahata chakra"), and the subtle dimension of the being

The "right side"—which is the "seat" of the causal dimension (or root-dimension) of the being (equivalent to the primal presumption that one exists as a separate "self", or "ego"), and which is (simultaneously) the "doorway" in the body-mind through which the ego can be utterly dissolved, in heart-Identification with Avatar Adi Da.

As the practice of Adidam matures, the progressive Spiritual activation of each of the three stations of the heart can be tangibly felt.

The Spiritual Initiation that Avatar Adi Da Gives to His fully prepared listening devotees is His Spiritual Activation of the left side of the heart, which (in due course) also becomes His Spiritual Activation of the middle station of the heart. Avatar Adi Da's Spiritual Gift of the Samadhi of the "Thumbs" is what makes possible His Spiritual Activation of the right side of the heart, which is coincident with the practitioner's entrance into the "Perfect Practice" of Adidam.

Because there is not a "downward-and-upward" quality to the three stations of the heart, Avatar Adi Da refers to them as the "horizontal" dimension of esoteric anatomy. A minority of the world's Spiritual traditions (principally certain branches of the Hindu, Buddhist, Jain, and Taoist traditions) are focused in processes that relate to the horizontal dimension (and especially the right side of the heart)—seeking, as an ultimate result, an "interiorly secluded" Identification with the Divine (or Realization of Truth). In the fullest development of this "horizontal" approach, the practitioner does, in fact, experience an Identification with the Divine (or a Realization of Truth) that is achieved by excluding all awareness of body and mind and world. Such exclusive Union with the Divine, however, is not permanent (or eternal), because it depends on the effort of the individual—the effort to "go within", or to exclude everything that is apparently objective. Thus, such exclusive Union with the Divine is not most perfect Divine Enlightenment. Rather, it is a matter of "choosing" the "Consciousness" aspect of the Divine—over the "Light" (or "Energy") aspect.

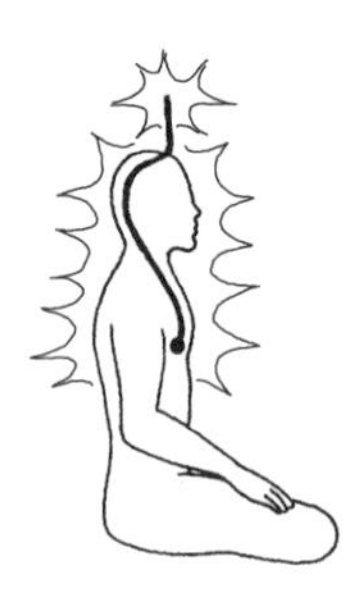

The <u>third</u> (and quintessential) <u>structure</u> of esoteric anatomy is what Avatar Adi Da calls "<u>Amrita</u> <u>Nadi</u>", using the traditional Sanskrit term (which means "Channel of Nectar"). Amrita Nadi is a radiant energy-structure, the "Bright" Itself as It Manifests in the context of the human body-mind. Amrita Nadi is shaped like the letter "S", extending from the right side of the heart (as its "lower terminal") through the chest, throat, and head, and then to the Source-Matrix of Divine Light infinitely above (as its "upper terminal"). Thus, Amrita Nadi encompasses both of the "locations" that have (in the most esoteric branches of the Great Tradition) been sought as the ultimate Divine "place"—the infinitely ascended Matrix of Light ("Above") and the right side of the heart ("within", or, more accurately, "Prior").

In the Great Tradition of religion and Spirituality, there have been two fundamental "camps"—the "vertical" and the "horizontal", or those who seek the Divine by going "up" and those who seek the Divine by going "within". What makes Avatar Adi Da's Revelation of the true world-religion of Adidam utterly unique is His "Disclosure" that, although both the vertical and the horizontal approaches are capable of resulting in a true glimpse of the Divine (or of Perfect Truth), <u>neither</u> the vertical <u>nor</u> the horizontal approach can lead to most perfect Divine Enlightenment (which is permanent, or eternal). Only the simultaneous Realization of the Divine in both "locations"—the infinitely ascended Source-Matrix of Divine Light and the right side of the heart (or both "terminals" of Amrita Nadi)—is most perfect (and eternal) Divine Enlightenment. Only the Full and Indivisible Realization of the Divine as Conscious Light (Consciousness and Light) is most perfect (and eternal) Divine Enlightenment. Such is the infinitely glorious Realization Given by Avatar Adi Da to His devotees who complete the entire process of the Way of Adidam. That Realization has never been known before Avatar Adi Da's Appearance in the world and His Gift of the Way of Adidam. Such is the culmination of the searchless process of simply Beholding Avatar Adi Da, the bodily (human) Incarnation of the "Bright" Itself.

Thus, Adidam is neither a "vertical" way nor a "horizontal" way. Rather, it is the unique "vertical-and-horizontal" Way. It is the Way of whole bodily Enlightenment, because it culminates in the Most Perfect Realization of the "whole body" of Amrita Nadi.

The "Perfect Practice"

Once you are Spiritually Initiated by Avatar Adi Da into the "Perfect Practice", you are free of identification with body and mind. Thus, the "Perfect Practice" is practice in the context of Consciousness Itself.

The "Perfect Practice" progresses through three stages. For each of these stages, Avatar Adi Da has Given a brief Admonition that epitomizes the essence of practice in that stage:

1. Be Consciousness (Itself).
2. Contemplate Consciousness (Itself).
3. Transcend everything in Consciousness (Itself).

It is important to understand, however, that this practice in the "realm" of Consciousness Itself is not a mental or philosophical exercise, not a form of "mind Dharma". Rather, the "Perfect Practice" of Adidam takes place entirely within the context of, and on the basis of, the devotional and Spiritual turning to Avatar Adi Da and fullest reception of His Ruchira Shaktipat, His Spiritual Transmission of the "Bright" Itself. Thus, the "Perfect Practice" encompasses—and goes beyond—everything that has ever been experienced or discovered in both the "vertical" (or Light-oriented) and the "horizontal" (or Consciousness-oriented) approaches to the Divine, and all of the first six stages of life.

At last, Avatar Adi Da's devotee is Spiritually Drawn by Him into the third stage of the "Perfect Practice", corresponding to the Admonition "Transcend everything In Consciousness (Itself)". This is the perfect fulfillment of both the "vertical" and the "horizontal" dimensions of the being. This is most perfect Divine Self-Realization, most perfect Awakening to the Divine Conscious Light, most perfect (and eternal) Divine Communion with Avatar Adi Da Samraj.

The Nature of Consciousness

Consciousness (Itself) Is That Which, when fully Realized, sets you Free from all bondage and all seeking.

Consciousness (Itself) Is Real God.

Consciousness (Itself) Is the Truth.

Consciousness (Itself) Is the Divine Liberator, Eleutherios.

—Avatar Adi Da Samraj
Eleutherios

The three stages of the "Perfect Practice"

Excerpts from
Eleutherios (The Only Truth That Sets The Heart Free)
by Avatar Adi Da Samraj

Be Consciousness (Itself).

This foundation stage (or prerequisite part) of the "Perfect Practice" of the only-by-Me Revealed and Given Way of Adidam is associated with a natural (or effortless) state of functional psycho-physical equanimity—such that functional energy and attention are free to dissolve (or be forgotten) in the by-Me-Revealed "Perfect Space" of Being (Itself), or Love-Bliss-Consciousness (Itself).

Contemplate Consciousness (Itself).

This middle stage (or intensively deepening counter-egoic exercise, and, thus, central part) of the "Perfect Practice" of the only-by-Me Revealed and Given Way of Adidam is complete when there is no longer the slightest feeling (or possibility) of doubt relative to the Divine Status of Consciousness (Itself)—As the Transcendental, and Inherently Spiritual (or Love-Blissful), and inherently egoless, and Self-Evidently Divine, and Perfectly Subjective Source (and Source-Condition) of the conditional self and of all of conditional Nature.

Transcend everything in Consciousness (Itself).

The fundamental characteristic of this final stage (or inherently egoless, and Truly Most Perfect part) of the "Perfect Practice" of the only-by-Me Revealed and Given Way of

Adidam is that there is no longer any ego-binding identification with the arising of functional attention, and no longer any ego-binding identification with any form of conditional self or conditional world—and this final stage (or part) of the "Perfect Practice" of the only-by-Me Revealed and Given Way of Adidam is complete (or most finally, and Most Perfectly, Demonstrated) when the totality of all (apparently) arising objects and limited (and limiting) conditions (and the root-feeling of relatedness itself, and even all of "difference") is Utterly Outshined By and In (and, Thus, Divinely Translated Into) My Avatarically Self-Revealed Love-Bliss-"Bright" Divine Self-Condition (and Divine "Bright" Spherical Self-Domain) of Perfectly Subjective (or Transcendental, Inherently Spiritual, Inherently egoless, and Self-Evidently Divine) Self-Existence.

Most Perfect Divine Self-Realization

Throughout its course, the Way of Adidam is always based on the devotional and Spiritual relationship to Avatar Adi Da Samraj, and an ever-deepening process of Communion with Him and reception of His Ruchira Shaktipat.

The culmination of this devotional and Spiritual Way, the third stage of the "Perfect Practice", is Divine Enlightenment—utter, permanent, and complete Identification with Avatar Adi Da's "Bright" Divine State. This Realization, as Demonstrated through the Life of Avatar Adi Da, is not any form of withdrawal from conditions and relations. Rather, it is the most Sublime and Profound Demonstration of Love-Bliss.

Avatar Adi Da describes this State of Divine Self-Realization, or Real-God-Realization, or Divine Enlightenment:

The Fundamental Current of Existence
Is Self-Existing,
Self-Radiant,

All-Love-Bliss—
and, Therefore,
All-Pleasure.

No self-suppression.
No ego-enforcing control whatsoever.

Consciousness Itself
and Energy Itself
(or Light Itself)
Are Love-Bliss Itself.

Love-Bliss Itself
Is Boundless—
not controlled at all,
not merely a "point".

Love-Bliss "Arises"
In Consciousness.
Consciousness Is the Room.
Love-Bliss Is all there is within It.
And the Room Is a Sphere. . . .

The Inherent Radiance
of Being
Is Bliss,
Freedom,
Happiness,
Fullness,
Un-conditional Well-Being.

This Is
Inherently The Case—
not merely the case
sometimes,
somewhere else,
after death.

The Inherent Radiance
of Being
Is the Condition
of existence.
Therefore,
the Integrity of Being
is to Realize This,
Always Already.
And sadhana is
everything in a life
done to Realize This,
Always Already—
until It Is
Self-Evidently Realized,
Always Already.

And then
There Is
Just That.
And That
Is That.

—Avatar Adi Da Samraj
The All-Completing and Final
Divine Revelation To Mankind

This is one of the many descriptions Avatar Adi Da has given of the most perfect Realization of the "Bright" that He has uniquely Brought into this world. The process of Awakening to His "Bright" Divine State (by means of His Divine Grace) is Ruchira Shaktipat Yoga, the progressively developing devotional and Spiritual relationship to Avatar Adi Da, the Divine Transmission-Master. Ruchira Shaktipat Yoga is the Fifth Fundamental of the True World-Religion of Adidam. ■

The Dual Sensitivity at the Origin of The Divine Way Of Adidam

from
The Only Complete Way To Realize The Unbroken Light Of Real God
by Avatar Adi Da Samraj

We conclude this chapter with a Discourse in which Avatar Adi Da discusses the profound necessity for a life of authentic religious and Spiritual practice—based on His very sobering assessment of our actual condition, and the ecstatic possibility of True Happiness in Communion with Him.

AVATAR ADI DA SAMRAJ: Merely by virtue of being born, you are in a terrible situation. Merely by virtue of being associated with a body-mind in this world, you are identified with bodily existence (and with conditional existence altogether), you are attached to bodily existence (and to conditional existence altogether), and you are clinging to bodily existence (and to conditional existence altogether). You know that the body is going to die—that it is not going to last, that it is going to go through all kinds of changes in its progress toward inevitable death, and that it can die at any moment. You know that the body can suffer tremendous losses, pain, shocks, degradation—of all kinds. And, yet, you (in your bodily existence here) are impulsed to be, and to be greatly—to be happy, to acquire this and that relationship or experience or object, to feel good, as if you were building a paradise.

Yet, you are not <u>in</u> paradise. You are in this mortal condition. Nothing you can acquire, obtain, or associate with in the realm of conditional experience will last. No matter what you seek, no matter what you obtain, your situation is still the same: From the point of view of "you" (as an apparently separate psycho-physical being), existence is just a knot of egoity, inevitably bound to suffer. Having no great Realization, you try to solve the "problem" (or the difficulty, or the terrible circumstance) in which you find yourself, by pursuing every kind of pleasure, consolation, and distraction. Moment by moment, you make efforts to desensitize yourself to the situation you are really in.

You are constantly fantasizing a future of fulfillment. Much of religious dogma invents a future, in this world or after death, wherein all the kinds of things you hope to obtain by struggle in this life are eternalized. Some like to philosophize about this world, saying that some great event (or even Man-made result or effect) is going to happen that will "utopianize" (or otherwise perfect and eternalize) life in this world. Some like to believe that everyone is going to be physically resurrected after death, such that life in this world will continue "forever". Others like to fantasize a future beyond this world, in which exactly the same thing happens—the eternalization of the self-fulfillment one has sought in this life.

No matter how (or in whatever form or manner) it is proposed, <u>complete</u> and <u>permanent</u> <u>self</u>-fulfillment, in this or any other conditionally manifested world, is merely an ego-based <u>illusion</u>—a mortal <u>fantasy</u>! It is <u>the</u> conventional religious fantasy—and it is also <u>the</u> ordinary human fantasy.

You all do this egoic fantasizing "in small". You may not presently be thinking about eternalizing this world (or going to an eternal place of pleasure in another world), but you are <u>always</u> <u>seeking</u> for <u>self</u>-fulfillment, for pleasure, for consolation, for every kind of egoically satisfying distraction—so that you will not be required to experience your real (mortal, threatened, and limited) situation. Effectively, in your self-consoling mind, you are always "creating" a "utopia" (or imagining a "heaven"), and entertaining the expectation that "everything" is going to turn out "wonderfully" and "forever". Some things may last for a while, and some things are more pleasurable than others, but (nevertheless) your real situation remains the same—mortal, threatened, and limited.

If you were not preoccupied with all the things you use to console and indulge yourself (functionally, relationally, practically, and so on)—if you were not preoccupied either with the search or with some (necessarily, temporary and limited) circumstance that gives you the illusion that you are satisfying yourself—you would inevitably become sensitized to your real situation. And, if you allowed yourself to be thus sensitized, you would, necessarily, become aware that you are afraid. Your situation, as the separate psycho-physical ego-"I", is (inherently) frightening. Of course, you do not want to experience fear, you do not want to experience loss, sorrow, and separation, you do not want to experience any lack of pleasure at all—you do not want to suffer. Yet, really, all of these unwanted conditions are inevitable. You are constantly seeking to fantasize a way out of your real situation—trying to desensitize yourself (mentally, emotionally, and physically) to your real situation. You (the presumed ego-"I") are always trying, struggling, efforting, or (in every psycho-physical manner) seeking to forget your real situation.

This is how you tend to use ordinary life. All the functions of existence could, instead, be put to the Great Purpose—but to do that requires counter-egoic (or ego-surrendering) sadhana. Because you are self-contracted in the face of all this suffering, you use everything to serve the ego's purpose to be relieved of its disturbance. Even imagination serves this purpose. You will use anything to desensitize yourself to your actual situation. You fantasize "enlightenment", you fantasize "heaven", you fantasize living "happily", "freely", and "forever", you fantasize having perfectly self-fulfilling sex (every day, and forever)—you constantly fantasize self-fulfillment in every form, manner, and degree. Such fantasies are part of the nonsense of your ordinary egoity—including your ordinary religiosity.

In the traditional setting, many individuals have seriously wondered about all of this, in the midst of this entirely mortal condition. Generally, it can be said that the analysis of life represented collectively by the total Great Tradition of mankind has two essential features that are complementary to one another.

On the one hand, it has been (and continues to be) observed by the "wise" (in the traditional setting) that, in this circumstance of conditional existence (in and of itself), there is no complete, final, perfect, and permanent self-satisfaction (or personal egoic happiness)—that no one and no thing lasts, every one and every thing changes, every one and every thing passes, and every one and every thing disintegrates (or dies).

On the other hand, it has also been noticed by the "wise" (in the traditional setting) that what the human being (and, indeed, even any being) wants is to be happy. To say so may sound rather trite or obvious, but it is fundamentally and profoundly true that all beings are urged to happiness—not merely to ordinary, temporary, and (necessarily) limited happiness, but to Ultimate, Perfect, Complete, and Permanent Happiness! Thus, it has been traditionally observed that True Happiness, if It is to be Really and Truly the Case, must be Unchanging, Unending, and utterly Satisfactory. This observation is the complement (and even the apparent contrary) of the first observation (that there is no complete, final, perfect, and permanent self-satisfaction, or personal egoic happiness, possible in the circumstance of conditional existence itself).

These complementary observations have always puzzled human beings. Here and there, great individuals have appeared who have confirmed, based on their own real experience, that There Is True Happiness, that There Is a Condition Which Is Eternal, Unchanging, Never-Ending, Never-Beginning, and (therefore) Not-Caused. That Condition has also been recognized (by such Realizers) to be All-Sufficient, Perfectly Satisfactory, Absolutely Blissful, and Infinite. That Condition has been (and is) called by various names—"the One", "God", "Nirvana", "the Self", and so on. And each of the many and various traditions has its own language for making reference to the Revelations and Confessions of those unique individuals who have, on the basis of actual Realization (and not mere hope and belief), Confessed the Truth of "True Happiness".

You are all seeking and suffering and binding yourselves in all kinds of ways—vigorously and obsessively trying to immunize yourselves against your difficulty and your inevitable pain, and not being very successful at it. You are merely "amateurs" at getting "What" you want. You do not really "Know" how to go about (or have the "Knowledge" that would Direct you Toward) getting "What" you want. And, what is more, you do not truly "Know" (or have the "Knowledge" that would Describe and Explain) "What" It Is That you want.

Truly, one of the words that most aptly indicates what you (and even every one) is seeking is "Happiness". You (at heart, and fully) want Happiness, although (in some sense) you would rather not even confess that Happiness is what you truly want—because you feel that the real attainment of Happiness is not even possible. Nevertheless, truly and always, this is what you want: Unalloyed, Unchanging, Absolute Happiness. The "problem", simply stated, is that you are not any good at "getting" It! And you do not "Know" What True Happiness Really Is. Therefore, you are in the same situation that the rest of ordinary humanity has been in all along.

I am not here merely to instruct you in how to improve your search, or how to be better at consoling yourself with illusions of True Happiness. I Am here to Speak and Do the most "radical" Criticism of what you (as an ego-"I") are always doing. I Call you to directly (and in every present-time moment) "Bond" yourself to True Happiness Itself, instead of (first and always) binding yourself to un-Happiness (and, on that basis, seeking for True Happiness). All your ordinary pursuits are an ego-based search that is moving in the opposite direction from the actual Realization of True Happiness—or the (necessarily, egoless) Realization of Truth, or Reality Itself, or the only Real God (Which Is the Non-Separate and Indivisible and Indestructible and Inherently egoless Divine Self-Condition and Source-Condition of all-and-All).

You, in the midst of this circumstance of mortality, are (simply) afraid—and you are always trying to console yourself, to feel better, to forget about the dreadful situation you feel you are in. However, you are also more than merely afraid—you want True Happiness. To want True Happiness is inherent in your heart, in your deepest disposition of body-mind. Yet, what you are always doing in this mortal circumstance is effectively (and, altogether, experientially) cutting you off from yielding to your inherent and great heart-Impulse (and from the fulfillment of that Impulse). Instead of (directly, moment to moment, and, at last, Most Perfectly) Realizing True Happiness, you are preoccupied with all kinds of activities that are consoling and temporarily pleasurizing, and (in that process) you are actively "forgetting" your fear (or covering it up, by becoming desensitized to conditional reality), and you are also (in your constant habit of self-consolation and self-indulgence) effectively forgetting (or covering up) your heart-Impulse to True Happiness Itself, Freedom Itself, and Love-Bliss Itself.

I Affirm and Confirm to you, on the Firm Basis of actual (and Eternal) Realization, that There Is the Infinite, Satisfactory, Unchanging, Eternal, Divine Condition, and that It Is the One and Only True Happiness—but I am not telling you that this world is going to turn into utopia, and I am also not telling you that what is merely "after death" is utopia (or that True Happiness is inevitable, or guaranteed, "after death").

In their ordinary religiosity, many people like to imagine that, when one dies, if one has been good, one receives back everything one lost by dying. Such people imagine that, after death, every one and every thing you ever positively wanted is permanently (and freshly) given back to you—all your relations and all the pleasures—and that every one and every thing you ever did not want is permanently removed from you. Indeed, it is commonly imagined that the so-called "after-life" is about such fulfillment of personal desires.

It is, indeed, the case that experiences can be attained, and relations can be associated with, under the many and various conditions that may arise after death, just as they can be experienced and associated with under the many and various conditions in this life—but (generally speaking) both the desired and the undesired experiences and relations are possible after death, and (in any case) none of it is permanent. In that respect, "life after death" is not a different circumstance than one's present life in the world. Just as in life, after death one's particular experiences and relations do not last. Just as in life, after death there are constant changes in your experience, new forms constantly arising, requiring a constant struggle. There is not anything finally Satisfactory, no True and Eternal Happiness, to be gained merely by the passage into the realms of "after-death".

Even the (so-called) "higher" planes—which do exist—are not about the eternalization of all the relations and things you wanted in this life. The "higher" planes are about Contemplation—the most profound movement toward What Is Beyond the ego-"I" and its conditional desiring. What *Is* (Inherently) Perfect is the right possible orientation (or occupation) in the "higher" planes, but (nevertheless) there is no permanent Satisfaction gained merely by existing and functioning and Contemplating in those planes.

The sadhana of the only-by-Me Revealed and Given Way of Adidam . . . requires you to be altogether *sensitive*—and *not* *desensitized*. The sadhana of the only-by-Me Revealed and Given Way of Adidam requires you to be sensitive to the reality of your mortal condition—and not merely to be consoling and indulging yourself, such that you manage to remain unaware of that reality. The sadhana of the only-by-Me Revealed and Given Way of Adidam also, and more profoundly, requires you to be sensitive to your inherent and great heart-Impulse—to be sensitive to the inherent deep awareness that you are not merely impulsed to be consoled, distracted, pleasurized, and self-indulgent, but that you are inherently and deeply and greatly Impulsed to be Truly and Infinitely Happy. You cannot be Really and Truly Happy when you are identified with something that is mortal, or changing, or unsatisfactory, or not-Happiness-Itself. This *dual* sensitivity—*both* to the *entirely* limited and mortal condition of your present psycho-physical form and circumstance *and* to the *inherent* and *great* heart-Impulse that would be Truly, Completely, and Un-conditionally Happy—is both necessary and *fundamental* to the practice of the only-by-Me Revealed and Given Way of Adidam. And the constant maintenance (or right use) of that dual sensitivity requires right devotion, right practice, right discipline, and truly (and not merely conventionally) right life.

The fundamental Principle of the only-by-Me Revealed and Given Way of Adidam is devotional recognition of Me and devotional response to Me—becoming, in due course, searchless Beholding (and Spiritual reception) of Me. I not only Confess the Truth to you, but I Am here. I Am the Very "Thing" I Confess, the Very (and True, or Un-conditional) Happiness you would Realize. And I Am (now, and forever hereafter) constantly Revealing and Giving Myself to you—to one, and to all, and to All. Therefore, the fundamental Principle of the Way of Adidam is to surrender yourself, forget yourself, and (always more and more) transcend yourself, in heart-Communion with Me. There must be this dual sensitivity I just Described, and the appropriate life-discipline to maintain that dual sensitivity. In that dual sensitivity, you must receive My Avataric Divine Self-Revelation and make the Eternal Vow of devotion to Me, such that your practice (moment to moment) is the commitment to True Happiness, the commitment to Realize Me—and not merely the oblivious "commitment" to wander in the searches and the results of your egoic (or self-contracted) impulses. . . .

I have exactly and fully Revealed the Way of True Happiness. It is the only-by-Me Revealed and Given Way of Adidam. That Way is not about any ordinary (or ego-based) binding of "self" to this world, or to any ego or any thing in this world, or to any limiting condition or conditional world at all. The only-by-Me Revealed and Given Way of Adidam is about heart-"Bonding" to Me—Which is heart-"Bonding" to Truth, or to Reality Itself, the One and Only and Non-Separate and Indivisible and Indestructible and Inherently egoless Divine Self-Condition and Source-Condition of all-and-All.

That Process of heart-"Bonding" to Me is done in the context of this apparent born existence, but it is a Process of always present-time (or non-seeking) ego-transcendence, or of constantly going Beyond your self-contracting (or separative, and seeking) disposition. This sadhana is a purifying Process. There is growth in it. The practice of the Way of Adidam is about devoting your life to always presently (and, at last, Most Perfectly) Realizing True Happiness, and not using up your life by remaining ego-bound, merely pursuing consolations and indulging in the illusion that "bonding" to what is merely conditionally existing can produce True Happiness. It cannot.

True Happiness (Itself) is not a result of anything. True Happiness (Itself) Is Inherent. Therefore, True Happiness (Itself) cannot be attained by seeking. True Happiness (Itself) Is the Divine Self-Condition and Source-Condition (Itself). Anything that appears merely as "object" (or merely as conditionally "other") is (necessarily) limited and (inevitably) passing. You cannot Realize True Happiness (Itself) by "bonding" yourself to any "object" (or anything that is merely "other"). And you cannot Realize True Happiness (Itself) by strategic renunciation of (or strategic dissociation from) any "object" (or anything that is merely "other").

True Happiness (Itself) Is Realized when the ego-"I" (that otherwise seeks) is itself transcended in its Ultimate (or Divine) Source. . . .

The only-by-Me Revealed and Given Way of Adidam neither idealizes nor merely consoles bodily-based (and egoic) existence, but the practice of the Way of Adidam requires the disciplining of bodily existence, from the very beginning (or foundation) of the Way. Therefore, by conforming all of your bodily existence to Me, by practicing right, true, and full (and, in due course, searchlessly Me-Beholding) devotion to Me, and by being psycho-physically purified through right, true, and full (and, in due course, searchlessly Me-Beholding) devotion to Me—you come to know Me better, and (more and more) in the truly esoteric (and truly Spiritual) manner, such that you grow to Commune with Me Spiritually (and truly Divinely), and (on that basis) you (in due course) move on to the (Spiritually) fully technically responsible stages of practice in the only-by-Me Revealed and Given Way of Adidam. . . .

It seems you have plenty of time! Indeed, you have nothing but time—and space! Over and over and over again. That is what is called "samsara" (or the endless cycle of rebirths). In samsara (or the conditional domain), there is a seemingly endless resource of time and space, but no resource at all of Real True Happiness. True Happiness (Itself) is the Greater Well, Beyond time and space. True Happiness (Itself) is the Divine Source, to Which you must resort directly. Only by resorting to the Divine Well of True Happiness (Itself) can you go Beyond this horror to which you are now bound.

You are mind, perpetuating a circumstance of bondage to what suffers and is limited and passes. You feel you can cope with that circumstance, you do not even mind it all that much, and you are willing to put up with it because you can acquire some pleasure in the midst of it. That is how you commit yourself to time and space. Yet, if you really do not like it, if you truly do not want to be conjoined with death, or with what is (altogether) not satisfactory, or with what is not True Happiness (Itself), or with what is changing (rather than Unchanging)—if you really and truly do not want to be bound to all of that (or even associated with all of that), it is not necessary for you to be thus bound (or associated). I Reveal and Give to you That Which Transcends all that is insufficient, unsatisfactory, and incomplete. By right, true, full, and fully devotional resort to Me, you can (and do, and will) Realize My

Avatarically Self-Revealed Infinite Divine Self-Condition of Absolute Love-Bliss-Happiness (Which Is True Happiness, Itself).

The Infinite Divine Self-Condition (or the Divine Well of True Happiness, Itself) Does Exist. I Am That. That Condition Is the Truth. That Condition Is Reality Itself.

You are, inherently, completely able to actively commit your life utterly to the Realization of Me, to the Realization of My Avatarically Self-Revealed (and Self-Evidently Divine) Self-Condition of Infinite Love-Bliss-Happiness, rather than to any other "program". By Means of My Avatarically Self-Transmitted Divine Spiritual Grace, you can (in due course) truly (and, Ultimately, Most Perfectly) fulfill that commitment. . . . By practicing the only-by-Me Revealed and Given discipline of devotion to Me, you will be more and more purified of those limitations. . . .

If you are My formally acknowledged and formally practicing devotee, you are no longer merely seeking Me, but you (in even every moment) have Found Me—the Avatarically Self-Revealed Divine Reality of True Happiness (Itself), and the Avatarically Self-Transmitted Divine Means for your Realization of True Happiness (Itself).

AN INVITATION

Becoming a Formal Devotee of Avatar Adi Da

Responding to the Revelation of the Eternal Divine Truth

Merely to be given the philosophy of mortality and materialism is an insult to the deepest intuitions of the human heart. And, yet, this is the message of the present global (and globalizing) Western culture. Avatar Adi Da Samraj has said:

> *The ego-"culture" of this "late-time" (or "dark" epoch) is all a play upon the most limited possible point of view: identification with the gross (physical) body—and, therefore, identification with a natural (or, otherwise, presumed) process that inevitably leads to death. The entire world of the "late-time" is bound to this philosophy of utter "darkness".*
>
> —Avatar Adi Da Samraj
> *Real God Is The Indivisible Oneness Of Unbroken Light*

No mere belief or hope can prove what lies beyond the ordinary perceptions, experiences, and sufferings of the world. But, as this book has demonstrated, the Ruchira Avatar, Adi Da Samraj, Reveals the height and depth of the One Spiritual Reality, of Which He is the living Incarnation. His Revelation satisfies the heart, even now.

Having discovered Avatar Adi Da Samraj and His Revelation, you are invited to enter into a devotional and Spiritual relationship to Him that will transform every moment of your existence into blissful Communion with the "Bright" Divine Person—inherently going beyond materialism and mortality.

This Divine Life is the Way of Adidam, uniquely Revealed by Avatar Adi Da by means of His own thirty-year Submission to humankind. Through total psycho-physical surrender, of body, mind, feeling, and breath to Him, He calls You to always newly discover and ultimately to most perfectly Realize Him—the supremely blissful, infinitely profound, inherently Radiant Divine Being and Condition that is your own native State, now and forever.

The Culture of Response to Avatar Adi Da

The responsive (and participatory, and ego-surrendering) disposition inherently transcends the body, and (thereby) inherently transcends death. In that case, a different kind of individual and collective human culture is made possible. That culture is the death-transcending culture of life itself—which is (necessarily) a culture of Spiritual practice, and (ultimately) the culture of Divine life.

—Avatar Adi Da Samraj
Real God Is The Indivisible Oneness Of Unbroken Light

The profound relationship to Avatar Adi Da is lived in the context of the worldwide gathering of His devotees. This gathering comprises a "Global Ashram"—the cooperative devotional culture of Adidam. Within this cooperative culture—which is lived with other practitioners of Adidam local to you, and unified with the entire Global Ashram of Adidam through all forms of modern communication—every individual devotee is able to grow and be accountable for his or her practice of the relationship to the Ruchira Avatar, Adi Da.

To find out how you can become a formal devotee of Avatar Adi Da and begin to practice the Way of Adidam, contact one of our centers, using the information given on the following pages.

What You Can Do Next—

Contact an Adidam center near you

- To find out about becoming a formal devotee of Avatar Adi Da, and for information about upcoming courses, events, and seminars in your area:

AMERICAS
12040 North Seigler Road
Middletown, CA 95461 USA
1-707-928-4936

PACIFIC-ASIA
12 Seibel Road
Henderson
Auckland 1008
New Zealand
64-9-838-9114

AUSTRALIA
P.O. Box 244
Kew 3101
Victoria
1800 ADIDAM
(1800-234-326)

EUROPE-AFRICA
Annendaalderweg 10
6105 AT Maria Hoop
The Netherlands
31 (0)20 468 1442

THE UNITED KINGDOM
PO Box 20013
London, England
NW2 1ZA
0208-962-8855

EMAIL:
correspondence@adidam.org

- For more contact information about local Adidam groups, please see **www.adidam.org/centers**

Learn more about
Avatar Adi Da Samraj and Adidam . . .
Visit ***www.adidam.org***

- **SEE AUDIO-VISUAL PRESENTATIONS** on the Divine Life and Spiritual Revelation of Avatar Adi Da Samraj
- **LISTEN TO DISCOURSES** Given by Avatar Adi Da Samraj to His practicing devotees—
  - Transcending egoic notions of God
  - Why Reality cannot be grasped by the mind
  - How the devotional relationship to Avatar Adi Da moves you beyond ego-bondage
  - The supreme process of Spiritual Transmission
- **HEAR DEVOTEES** of the Divine Avatar speaking about how He has transformed their lives
- **READ QUOTATIONS** from the "Source-Texts" of Avatar Adi Da Samraj—
  - Real God as the only Reality
  - The ancient practice of Guru-devotion
  - The two opposing life-strategies characteristic of the West and the East—and the way beyond both
  - The Prior Unity at the root of all that exists
  - The limits of scientific materialism
  - The true religion beyond all seeking
  - The esoteric structure of the human being
  - The real process of death and reincarnation
  - The nature of Divine Enlightenment
- **SUBSCRIBE** to the online Global Ashram Magazine

Learn more about Avatar Adi Da's Liberating Offering to all

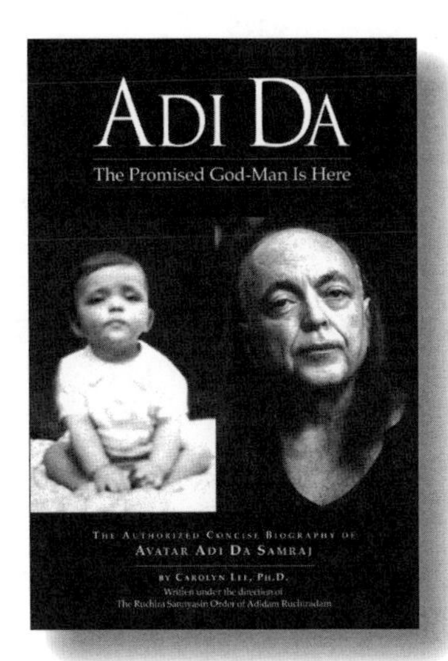

■ **ADI DA**
The Promised God-Man Is Here

The biography of Avatar Adi Da from His Birth to present time. Includes a wealth of quotations from His Writings and Talks, as well as stories told by His devotees. 358 pp., **$16.95**

This extraordinary book creates a powerful experience of the Reality and Truth of Ruchira Avatar Adi Da Samraj. Because it so poignantly quotes and clarifies His Teaching and His Life, it has deepened my experience of Him as the Divine Gift established in the cosmic domain.

—GABRIEL COUSENS, M.D.
Author, *Sevenfold Peace* and *Conscious Eating*

■ **ADI DA AND ADIDAM**
The Divine Self-Revelation of the Avataric Way of the "Bright" and the "Thumbs"

A 64-page introduction to Avatar Adi Da Samraj and His Unique Spiritual Revelation of the Way of Adidam.
$3.95

Read the Twenty-Three "Source-Texts" of Avatar Adi Da Samraj

In late 1969, in the brief period of three weeks, Avatar Adi Da wrote the original text of His literary masterwork, *The Mummery Book*. His writing of this book—which proved to be a remarkable prophecy of His Work to come—was the beginning of His immense Work of communicating His Revelation of Truth in words, both written and spoken. This outpouring lasted for 30 years, coming to a summary point in the years 1997–1999. During that period, Avatar Adi Da created a series of twenty-three books that He designated as His "Source-Texts". He incorporated into these books His most essential Writings and Discourses from all the preceding years, including many Writings and Discourses that had never been published previously. His "Source-Texts" are thus His Eternal Message to all. They contain His full Divine Self-Confession and His fully detailed description of the entire process of Awakening, culminating in seventh stage Divine Enlightenment.

Through the Revelation contained in His twenty-three "Source-Texts", Avatar Adi Da has brought to completion the search for Spiritual Truth that has occupied humankind for millennia. Looking at our current human situation in particular, He has demonstrated the untenability (and, indeed, the remarkable naivete, not to mention the negative influence) of the scientific materialist point of view, the point of view that (by asserting that the physical reality is the "only" and senior reality) creates an environment of doubt relative to everything beyond the physical domain—everything Divine, everything Spiritual, even everything psychic. And looking "back" at our entire history, He has "made sense" out of the welter of differing viewpoints in the Great

Tradition, demonstrating how they do, in fact, constitute a single (although complex) "design". And He has Made the Supreme Divine Offering that goes beyond what has ever been offered before—the Way that Realizes Permanent Indivisible Oneness with Him, the "Bright" Divine Reality Itself.

The twenty-three "Source-Texts" of Avatar Adi Da Samraj include:

- *The Dawn Horse Testament Of The Ruchira Avatar*
- *The Five Books Of The Heart Of The Adidam Revelation*
- *The Seventeen Companions Of The True Dawn Horse*

The Dawn Horse Testament

The Dawn Horse Testament
Of The Ruchira Avatar
The "Testament Of Secrets" Of The Divine World-Teacher, Ruchira Avatar Adi Da Samraj

Avatar Adi Da's paramount "Source-Text" is a complete summary of the entire Way of Adidam. It flows seamlessly from His Self-Revelation in the Prologue and chapter one; through a "consideration" of His Life and Work, expositions of His fundamental Teaching-Arguments and the fundamental practices He Gives to His devotees, and incisive descriptions of the egoic patterns of individual beings and human collectives; through the course of the stages of the Way of Adidam, culminating in seventh stage Divine Enlightenment; to the declaration of the Establishment of the Realization of the "Bright" and the Perpetual Revelation of the "Bright" via the Agency of His Work and Word and Person.

This Great Divine Testament is unparalleled in its magnitude and depth. No scripture like it has ever been seen before. It is the first and only complete account of the entire Divine Way of utter ego-transcendence and dissolution in the "Brightness" of Real God.

The Dawn Horse Testament is truly the core of Avatar Adi Da's twenty-three "Source-Texts". Indeed, all of the "Five Books" and most of the "Seventeen Companions" are built around a central text drawn from *The Dawn Horse Testament*.

The Five Books Of The Heart Of The Adidam Revelation

The Five Books Of The Heart Of The Adidam Revelation comprise a complete summary of Who Avatar Adi Da Samraj Is and the Way that He Offers. The "Five Books" are key readings for all who are moved to study the Essence of His Revelation and His Way.

BOOK ONE:
Aham Da Asmi
(Beloved, I Am Da)
The "Late-Time" Avataric Revelation Of The True and Spiritual Divine Person (The egoless Personal Presence Of Reality and Truth, Which Is The Only Real God)

Avatar Adi Da's Self-Revelation of His own Divine Person and His Impulse to Bless and Liberate all.

BOOK TWO:
Ruchira Avatara Gita
(The Avataric Way Of The Divine Heart-Master)
The "Late-Time" Avataric Revelation Of The Great Secret Of The Divinely Self-Revealed Way That Most Perfectly Realizes The True and Spiritual Divine Person (The egoless Personal Presence Of Reality and Truth, Which Is The Only Real God)

Avatar Adi Da's Offering of the devotional and Spiritual relationship to Him, in the traditional manner of Guru-devotion.

BOOK THREE:
Da Love-Ananda Gita
(The Free Gift Of The Divine Love-Bliss)
The "Late-Time" Avataric Revelation Of The Great Means To Worship and To Realize The True and Spiritual Divine Person (The egoless Personal Presence Of Reality and Truth, Which Is The Only Real God)

The foundation (devotional) practice of heart-Communion with Avatar Adi Da Samraj: Simply turning the four principal human faculties—body, emotion, mind, and breath—to Him.

BOOK FOUR:

Hridaya Rosary
(Four Thorns Of Heart-Instruction)

The "Late-Time" Avataric Revelation Of The Universally Tangible Divine Spiritual Body, Which Is The Supreme Agent Of The Great Means To Worship and To Realize The True and Spiritual Divine Person (The egoless Personal Presence Of Reality and Truth, Which Is The Only Real God)

The Spiritually Awakened practice of heart-Communion with Avatar Adi Da Samraj: Searchless Beholding of Him and reception of His Divine Spiritual Transmission—more and more allowing oneself to open Upwardly to Him, such that body, emotion, mind, and breath are "Melted" by His down-Flowing Spiritual Infusion.

BOOK FIVE:

Eleutherios
(The Only Truth That Sets The Heart Free)

The "Late-Time" Avataric Revelation Of The "Perfect Practice" Of The Great Means To Worship and To Realize The True and Spiritual Divine Person (The egoless Personal Presence Of Reality and Truth, Which Is The Only Real God)

Heart-Communion with Avatar Adi Da Samraj beyond the four faculties, in the Domain of Consciousness Itself: Realizing Avatar Adi Da Samraj—As the "Bright" Itself, or the Conscious Light of Reality (having transcended identification with body, emotion, mind, and breath).

The Seventeen Companions Of The True Dawn Horse

The "True Dawn Horse" is a reference to *The Dawn Horse Testament Of The Ruchira Avatar.* Each of *The Seventeen Companions Of The True Dawn Horse* is a "Companion" to *The Dawn Horse Testament* in the sense that it is an elaboration of a principal theme (or a group of principal themes) from *The Dawn Horse Testament.* Among the "Seventeen Companions" are included Avatar Adi Da's two tellings of His own Life-Story, as autobiography (*The Knee Of Listening*) and as archetypal parable (*The Mummery Book*).

The Seventeen Companions Of The True Dawn Horse are a vast field of Revelation, which can be "considered" from many points of view. Presented here is one way of understanding the interrelationships between these "Source-Texts" and the flow of Argument they collectively represent.

Paradigms of Reality:
The Real Nature of God, Cosmos, and Realization

BOOK ONE:

Real God Is The Indivisible Oneness Of Unbroken Light

Reality, Truth, and The "Non-Creator" God In The True World-Religion Of Adidam

The Nature of Real God and the nature of the cosmos. Why ultimate questions cannot be answered either by conventional religion or by science.

BOOK TWO:

The Truly Human New World-Culture Of Unbroken Real-God-Man

The Eastern Versus The Western Traditional Cultures Of Mankind, and The Unique New Non-Dual Culture Of The True World-Religion Of Adidam

The Eastern and Western approaches to religion, and to life altogether—and how the Way of Adidam goes beyond this apparent dichotomy.

BOOK THREE:

The Only Complete Way To Realize The Unbroken Light Of Real God

An Introductory Overview Of The "Radical" Divine Way Of The True World-Religion Of Adidam

The entire course of the Way of Adidam—the unique principles underlying Adidam, and the unique culmination of Adidam in Divine Enlightenment.

Original Writings and Talks:

Avatar Adi Da's First Teaching-Communications

BOOK FOUR:

The Knee Of Listening

The Divine Ordeal Of The Avataric Incarnation Of Conscious Light—The Spiritual Autobiography Of The Divine World-Teacher, Ruchira Avatar Adi Da Samraj

Avatar Adi Da's autobiographical account of the years from His Birth to His Divine Re-Awakening in 1970—His Demonstration, in His own Life, of the Way to Realize Real God most perfectly—also including His Revelation of how His Avataric Incarnation was made possible and His Confession of the nature and significance of the Great Events of Yogic Death that have occurred in His Life since His Divine Re-Awakening in 1970.

BOOK FIVE:

The Divine Siddha-Method Of The Ruchira Avatar

The Divine Way Of Adidam Is An ego-Transcending Relationship, Not An ego-Centric Technique

Avatar Adi Da's earliest Talks to His devotees, on the fundamental principles of the devotional relationship to Him and "radical" understanding of the ego. Accompanied by His summary statements on His relationship to Swami Muktananda and on His own unique Teaching-Work and Blessing-Work.

Book Six:
The Mummery Book
A Parable Of The Divine True Love, Told By Means Of A Self-Illuminated Illustration Of The Totality Of Mind

Avatar Adi Da's literary masterpiece—a work of astonishing poetry and deeply evocative archetypal drama. It is Avatar Adi Da's life-transforming message about how to Realize the Absolute Truth in the midst of the chaos and tragedy of human experience.

An extraordinarily beautiful and potent "prose opera", *The Mummery Book* is both a highly experimental novel (drawing fully on the twentieth-century "stream" of experimental fiction) and an immense theatrical piece. Thus, *The Mummery Book* can either be read as a book or performed as a theatrical event.

A "mummery" is "a ridiculous, hypocritical, or pretentious ceremony or performance". This, Avatar Adi Da is telling us, is what human life amounts to—if we merely live as the separate ego-self. And the only way "out" of this mummery is to relinquish ego—by finding, receiving, and conforming ourselves to the Divine True Love.

In *The Mummery Book*, Adi Da confronts head-on the central agony of born existence: that everything and everyone—ourselves, and everyone we love—dies. The hero of *The Mummery Book*, Raymond Darling, goes through an extraordinary series of adventures and ordeals—centered around his search for his beloved, a lady named Quandra—in the course of his ultimate overcoming of the inescapable fact of mortality. The story of Raymond Darling is, in fact, Avatar Adi Da's telling of His own Life-Story in the language of parable—including His unflinching portrayal of how the unconverted ego makes religion (and life altogether) into a meaningless mummery. Ultimately, *The Mummery Book* is the "Story" of Consciousness Realizing Its Indivisible Oneness with Energy (or Its own Radiance).

Esoteric Principles and Practices:
Revelations of Divine Oneness, Divine Spiritual Transmission, and the means of conforming the body-mind to the Divine Spiritual Process

BOOK SEVEN:

He-and-She Is Me

The Indivisibility Of Consciousness and Light In The Divine Body Of The Ruchira Avatar

One of Avatar Adi Da's most esoteric Revelations—His Primary "Incarnation" in the Cosmic domain as the "He" of the Divine Consciousness, the "She" of the Divine Light, and the "Son" of "He" and "She" in the "Me" of His Divine Spiritual Body.

BOOK EIGHT:

Ruchira Shaktipat Yoga

The Divine (and Not Merely Cosmic) Spiritual Baptism In The Divine Way Of Adidam

The Divine Heart-Power (Ruchira Shakti) uniquely Transmitted by Avatar Adi Da Samraj, and how it differs from the various traditional forms of Spiritual Baptism, particularly Kundalini Yoga.

BOOK NINE:

Ruchira Tantra Yoga

The Physical-Spiritual (and Truly Religious) Method Of Mental, Emotional, Sexual, and Whole Bodily Health and Enlightenment In The Divine Way Of Adidam

The transformation of life in the realms of money, food, and sex. Includes: understanding "victim-consciousness"; the ego as addict; the secret of how to change; going beyond the "Oedipal" sufferings of childhood; the right orientation to money; right diet; life-positive and Spiritually auspicious sexual practice, and so on.

Stages of Life:
The six potential stages of ego-based life, and the Divine seventh stage of life

BOOK TEN:
The Seven Stages Of Life
Transcending The Six Stages Of egoic Life, and Realizing The ego-Transcending Seventh Stage Of Life, In The Divine Way Of Adidam

The stages of human development from birth to Divine Enlightenment. How the stages relate to physical and esoteric anatomy. The errors of each of the first six stages of life, and the unique egolessness of the seventh stage of life. Avatar Adi Da's Self-Confession as the first, last, and only seventh stage Adept-Realizer.

BOOK ELEVEN:
The All-Completing and Final Divine Revelation To Mankind
A Summary Description Of The Supreme Yoga Of The Seventh Stage Of Life In The Divine Way Of Adidam

The ultimate secrets of Divine Enlightenment—including the four-stage Process of Divine Enlightenment, culminating in Translation into the Infinitely Love-Blissful Divine Self-Domain.

Process of Adidam:
Five Comprehensive Views of the Practice of Adidam

BOOK TWELVE:
What, Where, When, How, Why, and Who To Remember To Be Happy
A Simple Explanation Of The Divine Way Of Adidam (For Children, and Everyone Else)

A text written specifically for children but inspiring to all—with accompanying Essays and Talks on Divine Ignorance, religious practices for children and young people in the Way of Adidam, and the fundamental practice of whole bodily devotion to Avatar Adi Da Samraj.

BOOK THIRTEEN:
No Seeking / Mere Beholding
The Always Primary Practice Of The Divine Way Of Adidam

A comprehensive summary of the always primary practice of the Way of Adidam—which is searchless Beholding of Avatar Adi Da Samraj—including detailed Instruction relative to rightly participating in the unique opportunity of retreat in Avatar Adi Da's physical Company.

BOOK FOURTEEN:
Santosha Adidam
The Essential Summary Of The Divine Way Of Adidam

An extended overview of the entire course of the Way of Adidam, based on the esoteric anatomy of the human being and its correlation to the progressive stages of life.

BOOK FIFTEEN:
The Lion Sutra
The "Perfect Practice" Teachings In The Divine Way Of Adidam

Practice in the ultimate stages of the Way of Adidam. How the practitioner of Adidam approaches—and passes over—the "Threshold" of Divine Enlightenment.

BOOK SIXTEEN:
The Overnight Revelation Of Conscious Light
The "My House" Discourses On The Indivisible Tantra Of Adidam

A vast and profound "consideration" of the fundamental Tantric principles of true Spiritual life and the "Always Already" Nature of the Divine Reality.

Great Tradition:
The Total Spiritual "Effort" of Humanity as a Unified (and Progressive) Process

BOOK SEVENTEEN:

The Basket Of Tolerance

The Perfect Guide To Perfectly Unified Understanding Of The One and Great Tradition Of Mankind, and Of The Divine Way Of Adidam As The Perfect Completing Of The One and Great Tradition Of Mankind

The Basket Of Tolerance is a book like no other—simultaneously an unprecedented Spiritual Revelation and an extraordinary intellectual document.

While Avatar Adi Da's other twenty-two "Source-Texts" are focused in His exposition of the Way of Adidam, *The Basket Of Tolerance* is His comprehensive examination of the Great Tradition of mankind—in other words, of the global and historical context within which He has made His Revelation of the Way of Adidam. Thus, *The Basket Of Tolerance* focuses on the immense variety of historical expressions of the religious and Spiritual search, from prehistoric times to the present.

The core of *The Basket Of Tolerance* is a bibliographical listing of 5,000 documents (in all media—print and audio-visual), meticulously ordered by Avatar Adi Da in an elaborately subdivided sequence, to form a continuous "Argument". Avatar Adi Da introduces that "Argument" with a series of groundbreaking Essays, and He comments on the bibliographical "Argument", at numerous points, through a further series of over 100 essays relating to specific books (or groups of books) in the bibliography (covering a wide spectrum of topics).

Through the "Argument" of this annotated bibliography, Avatar Adi Da examines in detail the entire human religious search and demonstrates how there is truly a single process, composed of distinct (hierarchically related) stages (corresponding to the fourth, the fifth, and the sixth stages of life), evident in all the diversity of human religious history (previous to His Appearance here)—a process of which any given religious tradition represents a "piece". While Avatar Adi Da's examination of the Great Tradition concentrates on the various global manifestations of religion and Spirituality, it also embraces the "practical" issues that relate to the human process of the first three stages of life—such as understanding (and right participation in the process) of death, understanding (and right use) of the function of mind, right circulation of energy within the body, right physical exercise of the body, right diet, right emotional-sexual practice (whether sexually active or celibate), right living in the collective human context, and so forth.

Altogether, *The Basket Of Tolerance* is the elaborately detailed "proof" that there is, indeed, a "perennial philosophy". This "philosophy", however, is not a single "set" of unified "beliefs". Rather, it is a process, composed of distinctly different stages—and the points of view of the successive stages do not necessarily agree with one another. Furthermore, those stages are not (ultimately) based on conceptual differences but on experiential differences relating to the various aspects of the esoteric anatomy of the human structure.

Study other books and recordings by and about Avatar Adi Da Samraj

■ To find out about and order "Source-Texts", books, tapes, CDs, and videos by and about Avatar Adi Da, contact your local Adidam regional center, or contact the Adidam Emporium at:

1-877-770-0772 (from within North America)
1-707-928-6653 (from outside North America)

Or order online from: **www.dawnhorsepress.com**

Support Avatar Adi Da's Work and the Way of Adidam

■ If you are moved to serve Avatar Adi Da's Spiritual Work specifically through advocacy and/or financial patronage, please contact:

Advocacy
P.O. Box 204
Lower Lake, CA 95457
phone: (707) 928-4800
email: adidam_advocacy@adidam.org

For young people: Join the Adidam Youth Fellowship

■ Young people under 21 can participate in the "Adidam Youth Fellowship"—either as a friend or practicing member. Adidam Youth Fellowship members participate in study programs, retreats, celebrations, and other events with other young people responding to Avatar Adi Da. To learn more about the Youth Fellowship, call or write:

Vision of Mulund Institute (VMI)
10336 Loch Lomond Road, PMB 146
Middletown, CA 95461
phone: (707) 928-6932
fax: (707) 928-5619
email: vmi@adidam.org

The Ruchira Sannyasin Hermitage Ashrams Spiritually Empowered by Avatar Adi Da Samraj

Traditionally, Realizers have been provided with set-apart places where they were free to do their Spiritual Work in an appropriate and secluded circumstance. And these places became Spiritually Empowered through their Presence and Work.

In this traditional manner, devotees of Avatar Adi Da have provided places where He is completely set apart to do His Blessing-Work for the sake of humanity as a whole, as well as His specific Spiritual Work with devotees who come on pilgrimage to receive the Initiatory Spiritual Blessing of being in His physical Company on retreat.

My Work for the entire world is My Divine Blessing-Work, Which I do principally in seclusion. I live in perpetual retreat in a hermitage mode, and receive those of My devotees who are rightly prepared in that circumstance. Sometimes I roam in public circumstances, in order to have contact with people in general. But, fundamentally, I remain in hermitage retreat.

—Avatar Adi Da Samraj

Avatar Adi Da Samraj moves among the various Hermitage Ashrams in His spontaneous Wandering-Work of world-Blessing.

Spiritually, He is perpetually "in residence" at each of His Hermitage Sanctuaries. This is because He has Invested Himself Spiritually in these sacred places, and His Spiritual Power and Presence is constantly active in all of them.

Adidam Samrajashram
the Island of Naitauba in Fiji

Adidam Samrajashram is Avatar Adi Da's principal Hermitage Ashram and the primary Seat from which His Divine Spiritual Blessing Flows to the entire world.

The Mountain Of Attention Sanctuary of Adidam
in northern California

Da Love-Ananda Mahal
in Hawaii

An Invitation to Support Adidam

The sole Purpose of Avatar Adi Da Samraj is to act as a Source of continuous Divine Grace for everyone, everywhere. In that spirit, He is a Free Renunciate and He owns nothing. Those who have made gestures in support of Avatar Adi Da's Work have found that their generosity is returned in many Blessings that are full of His healing, transforming, and Liberating Grace and those Blessings flow not only directly to them as the beneficiaries of His Work, but to many others, even all others. At the same time, all tangible gifts of support help secure and nurture Avatar Adi Da's Work in necessary and practical ways, again similarly benefiting the entire world. Because all this is so, supporting His Work is the most auspicious form of financial giving, and we happily extend to you an invitation to serve Adidam through your financial support.

You may make a financial contribution in support of the Work of Adi Da Samraj at any time. To do so, make your check payable to "Adidam", and mail it to the Legal Department of Adidam at 12180 Ridge Road, Middletown, California 95461, USA. You may also, if you choose, indicate that your contribution be used for one or more specific purposes.

If you would like more detailed information about gifting options, or if you would like assistance in describing or making a contribution, please write to the Legal Department of Adidam at the above address or contact the Adidam Legal Department by telephone at 1-707-928-4612 or by FAX at 1-707-928-4062.

Planned Giving

We also invite you to consider making a planned gift in support of the Work of Avatar Adi Da Samraj. Many have found that through planned giving they can make a far more significant gesture of support than they would otherwise be able to make. Many have also found that by making a planned gift they are able to realize substantial tax advantages.

There are numerous ways to make a planned gift, including making a gift in your Will, or in your life insurance, or in a charitable trust.

If you are a United States taxpayer, you may find that planned giving in the form of a charitable trust will provide you with immediate tax savings and assured income for life, while at the same time enabling you to provide for your family, for your other heirs, and for the Work of Avatar Adi Da as well.

The Legal Department of Adidam (12180 Ridge Road, Middletown, California 95461, USA; telephone 1-707-928-4612; FAX 1-707-928-4062) will be happy to provide you with further information about these and other planned gifting options, and happy to provide you or your attorney with assistance in describing or making a planned gift in support of the Work of Avatar Adi Da.

Further Notes to the Reader

An Invitation to Responsibility

Adidam, the Way of the Heart that Avatar Adi Da has Revealed, is an invitation to everyone to assume real responsibility for his or her life. As Avatar Adi Da has Said in *The Dawn Horse Testament Of The Ruchira Avatar,* "If any one Is Heart-Moved To Realize Me, Let him or her First Resort (Formally, and By Formal Heart-Vow) To Me, and (Thereby) Commence The Devotional (and, In Due Course, Spiritual) Process Of self-Observation, self-Understanding, and self-Transcendence. . . ." Therefore, participation in the Way of Adidam requires a real confrontation with oneself, and not at all a confrontation with Avatar Adi Da, or with others.

All who study the Way of Adidam or take up its practice should remember that they are responding to a Call to become responsible for themselves. They should understand that they, not Avatar Adi Da or others, are responsible for any decision they may make or action they may take in the course of their lives of study or practice. This has always been true, and it is true whatever the individual's involvement in the Way of Adidam, be it as one who has contacted Avatar Adi Da's Revelation in any informal manner (such as studying Avatar Adi Da's Wisdom-Teaching), or as one who is practicing as a formally acknowledged congregational member of Adidam.

Honoring and Protecting the Sacred Word through Perpetual Copyright

Since ancient times, practitioners of true religion and Spirituality have valued, above all, time spent in the Company of the Sat-Guru (or one who has, to any degree, Realized Real God, Truth, or Reality, and who, thus, serves the awakening process in others). Such practitioners understand that the Sat-Guru literally Spiritually Transmits his or her (Realized) State. Through this Transmission, there are objects, environments, and rightly prepared individuals with which the Sat-Guru has contact that can become empowered, or imbued with the Sat-Guru's Transforming Power. It is by this process of empowerment that things and beings are made truly and literally sacred and holy, and things so sanctified thereafter function as a source of the Sat-Guru's Blessing for all who understand how to make right and sacred use of them.

Sat-Gurus of any degree of Realization and all that they empower are, therefore, truly Sacred Treasures, for they help draw the practitioner more quickly into the process of Realization. Cultures of true Wisdom have always understood that such Sacred Treasures are precious (and fragile) Gifts to humanity, and that they should be honored, protected, and reserved for right sacred use. Indeed, the word "holy" means "set apart", and, thus, that which is holy and sacred must be protected from insensitive secular interference and wrong use of any kind.

Avatar Adi Da has Conformed His human Body-Mind Most Perfectly to the Divine Self, and He is, thus, the most Potent Source of Spiritual Blessing-Transmission of Real God, or Truth Itself, or Reality Itself. He has for many years Empowered (or made sacred) special places and things, and these now serve as His Divine Agents, or as literal expressions and extensions of His Blessing-Transmission. Among these Empowered Sacred Treasures are His Wisdom-Teaching and His Divine Image-Art, which are full of His Transforming Power. These Blessed and Blessing Agents have the literal Power to serve Real-God-Realization in those who are Graced to receive them.

Therefore, Avatar Adi Da's Wisdom-Teaching and Divine Image-Art must be perpetually honored and protected, "set apart" from all possible interference and wrong use. The gathering of devotees of Avatar Adi Da is committed to the perpetual preservation and right honoring of the Sacred Wisdom-Teaching of the Way of Adidam and the Divine Image-Art of Adi Da Samraj. But it is also true that, in order to fully accomplish this, we must find support in the world-society in which we live and in its laws. Thus, we call for a world-society and for laws that acknowledge the sacred, and that permanently protect it from insensitive, secular interference and wrong use of any kind. We call for, among other things, a system of law that acknowledges that the Wisdom-Teaching of the Way of Adidam and the Divine Image-Art of Adi Da Samraj, in all their forms, are, because of their sacred nature, protected by perpetual copyright.

We invite others who respect the sacred to join with us in this call and in working toward its realization. And, even in the meantime, we claim that all copyrights to the Wisdom-Teaching and Divine Image-Art of Avatar Adi Da and the other Sacred Literature, recordings, and images of the Way of Adidam are of perpetual duration.

We make this claim on behalf of The Avataric Samrajya of Adidam Pty Ltd, which, acting as trustee of The Avataric Samrajya of Adidam, is the holder of all such copyrights.

Avatar Adi Da and the Sacred Treasures of Adidam

True Spiritual Masters have Realized Real God (to one degree or another), and, therefore, they bring great Blessing and introduce Divine Possibility to the world. Such Adept-Realizers Accomplish universal Blessing-Work that benefits everything and everyone. They also Work very specifically and intentionally with individuals who approach them as their devotees, and with those places where they reside and to which they direct their specific Regard for the sake of perpetual Spiritual Empowerment. This was understood in traditional Spiritual cultures, and, therefore, those cultures found ways to honor Adept-Realizers by providing circumstances for them where they were free to do their Spiritual Work without obstruction or interference.

Those who value Avatar Adi Da's Realization and Service have always endeavored to appropriately honor Him in this traditional way by providing a circumstance where He is completely Free to do His Divine Work. The Ruchira Sannyasin Hermitage Ashrams of Adidam have been set aside by Avatar Adi Da's devotees worldwide as Places for Him to do His universal Blessing-Work for the sake of everyone, as well as His specific Work with those who pilgrimage to His Hermitage circumstance (wherever He may be residing at a given time) to receive the special Blessing of coming into His physical Company.

Avatar Adi Da is a legal renunciate. He owns nothing and He has no secular or religious institutional function. He Functions only in Freedom. He, and the other members of the Ruchira Sannyasin Order (the senior renunciate order of Adidam), are provided for by The Avataric Samrajya of Adidam, which also provides for His Hermitage circumstance, and serves and manages the process of access to Avatar Adi Da Samraj on the part of all who are invited to enter His Hermitage Domain (either to offer service to Him or to participate in meditative retreats in His Spiritual Company).

The sacred institutions that have developed in response to Avatar Adi Da's Wisdom-Teaching and universal Blessing are active worldwide in making Avatar Adi Da's Wisdom-Teaching available to all, in offering guidance to all who are moved to respond to His Offering, and in protecting, preserving, and glorifying the Sacred Treasures of Adidam. In addition to the central corporate entities, which are based in California, there are numerous regional entities which serve congregations of Avatar Adi Da's devotees in various places throughout the world.

Practitioners of Adidam worldwide have also established numerous community organizations, through which they provide for many of their common and cooperative community needs, including those relating to housing, food, businesses, medical care, schools, and death and dying. By attending to these and all other ordinary human concerns and affairs via ego-transcending cooperation and mutual effort, Avatar Adi Da's devotees constantly work to free their energy and attention, both personally and collectively, for practice of the Way of Adidam and for service to Avatar Adi Da Samraj, to the other Sacred Treasures of Adidam, and to the sacred institutions of Adidam.

All of the organizations that have evolved in response to Avatar Adi Da Samraj and His Offering are legally separate from one another, and each has its own purpose and function. These organizations represent the collective intention of practitioners of Adidam worldwide to protect, preserve, and glorify the Sacred Treasures of Adidam, and also to make Avatar Adi Da's Offering of the Way of Adidam universally available to all.

Index